Dalton Plan:
Origins and Theory
of Dalton Education

Dalton Plan:
Origins and Theory of Dalton Education

Piet van der Ploeg

Saxion Dalton
University Press

Colophon
2020©   Piet van der Ploeg / Saxion Dalton University Press
Author   Piet van der Ploeg
Publisher   Saxion Dalton University Press
ISBN   9789490239022

No part of this book shall be reproduced, stored in a retrieval system or transmitted by any means, electronic, mechanical, photocopying, recording, or otherwise, without the prior written permission from the authors and publisher.

Book can be purchased as a printed book, eBook and streaming book in all (Web)Bookshops. For instance: Amazon.com, Bol.com and KOBO

Contents

	Introduction	6
1.	Practical origins	9
2.	The theory of the Dalton Plan	24
3.	Emerson	33
4.	Conklin	43
5.	Swift	50
6.	Dewey	65
7.	Montessori	89
8.	Taylor and Bobbitt	113
9.	The theory revisited	121
	References	137

Introduction

Apart from John Dewey, no American educational reformer has been as internationally successful and influential as Helen Parkhurst, the founder of Dalton education. In the twenties and thirties of the twentieth century, Dalton education was spread throughout the world. There is no certainty regarding the exact numbers of Dalton schools, but there was Dalton education in America, England, Germany, the Netherlands, the Soviet Union, India, China and Japan. Particularly in the Netherlands and Japan, Dalton education has remained in existence. In recent years there has been a revival of international interest. It crops up again, for instance, in England, Germany, the Czech Republic and Slovakia.

The Netherlands is the country with the highest density of Dalton schools. At the moment there are four hundred, three hundred and seventy of which are elementary schools. Comprising five percent of all elementary schools, Dalton education is by far the largest educational reform movement in the Netherlands. And, contrary to Montessori, Jena Plan and Waldorf education, it is steadily on the increase: approximately one hundred schools have been founded in the past five years. The only Dalton school in America, is the school that Helen Parkhurst founded herself in 1919, and which she was subsequently to direct for more than twenty years: the Dalton School in New York. It is a renowned school. But its fame is not due to its origins as an experiment in progressive education. The Dalton School is the second most expensive private school in New York.

There is no historical-theoretical literature available on the Dalton Plan as an educational concept. There are several studies in English concentrating on certain Dalton schools, among others the Dalton School in New York (by Semel: The Daltonschool. The Transformation of a Progressive School, 1992) and the King Alfred School in London (by Brooks: 'In a world set apart: The Dalton dynasty at King Alfred School, 1920-1960' in History of Education, 1998) and there is biography of Parkhurst (by Lager: Helen Parkhurst and the Dalton Plan: The Life and Work of an American Educator, 1983). The remaining literature on Dalton education in the English language is practically oriented and enthusiastic in tone, for instance The Dalton Laboratory Plan from 1922 by Evelyn Dewey (the daughter of John Dewey) and The Triumph of the Dalton Plan from 1924 by Kimmins and Rennie.

Perhaps the lack of historical-theoretical literature on Dalton education has something to do with both Parkhurst's practical nature and the pragmatic interest of Dalton teachers and others in Dalton circles. Parkhurst was herself not keen on theoretical exercises and theory was not her forte, as we shall see later on. In this study we hope to make plausible that historical-theoretical research is interesting nonetheless. It teaches us, for instance, that learning by experience or learning by doing doesn't mean the same and doesn't have the same role in Parkhurst's case as it does for other education reformers; what the difference is between working with assignments in the Dalton Plan and working with materials in the Montessori Method; that the Dalton Plan holds efficiency as its main objective, whilst at the same time opposing head-on the efficiency-hype seen at the beginning of the twentieth century; it teaches us the meaning of cooperation in original Dalton education and how much this differs from what we usually mean by this; in which sense Parkhurst's school as a working community distinguishes itself from that of Dewey; what freedom is in the Dalton Plan and why it is not the same as freedom of choice; how Parkhurst steers away from discussions centering on subject matter and the curriculum, and why this is inconsistent.

Such matters hold practical significance. An adequate and detailed depiction of the original theory of the Dalton Plan, its background, the traditions to which the theory is related and to which it runs counter, is for instance required when the identity of Dalton education is under discussion (what actually is Dalton education, what's its essence, where are the boundaries, what is no longer Dalton, what is misconstrued Dalton?), when we wish to know just what distinguishes Dalton education from other innovative forms of education and educational reform (what's the difference between Dalton and Jena Plan or Montessori and what's the difference between Dalton education and discovery learning or self-guided learning?) and when Dalton schools are in doubt as to how react to new developments in (school education and education in the broadest sense of the word) education, in society and culture and in science and technology.

We begin with an account of the original practice and theory of the Dalton Plan. The first chapter is mostly historical: a concise reconstruction of the history of the development of the Dalton Plan. The second chapter characterizes the theory of the Dalton Plan based upon our interpretation of texts written by Parkhurst. Then, we proceed to create a more in-depth and enriched picture by discussing, in the six following chapters, the theoretical background and context of the Dalton Plan and by comparing the Dalton Plan to other critical and innovative approaches to education. Tied in with all this, we then give a more detailed, extensive and refined characterization of the theory of the Dalton Plan.

Parkhurst's book Education on the Dalton Plan from 1922 is an important primary source in our research. We use the fourth edition published in 1926. The page numbering varies in the different printings. The version we consulted is available online via www.archive.org (direct link):

http://www.archive.org/details/educationondalto00parkiala

1 Practical origins

Dalton education is originally the work of Helen Parkhurst. Based on her biography[1] it is possible to reconstruct how the Dalton Plan came into existence and how it developed. The process actually began during her school years around 1900, and in this development two stages may be distinguished, both taking place early on in her teaching career. In 1912 the Dalton Plan is practically ready, although, at this time, it is not yet known by that name. Almost ten years pass before Parkhurst writes about it for the first time.

Own schooldays

Dalton education has its roots in Parkhurst's own schooldays. As a child and adolescent Helen had been bored to tears at school and she felt that she was not taken seriously. That is by no means surprising. She was born in 1886, and therefore went to school around the turn of the century: the closing years of the nineteenth century, the early twentieth century. At that time, American education was monotonous and one-sided; learning was dull and a matter of routine. There was little to capture the pupils' interest and not much for them to do: partly they were required to sit still and listen and partly they had to learn and recite facts by heart; nothing else. Most of the time the teacher was speaking: telling, explaining and asking questions. His questions were not intended to stimulate the pupils to think or start working, but to check whether they had remembered and could reproduce what they had been told or what they had read. Often the questioning was meant to prompt the whole class to simultaneously grind out ready-made, recently memorized facts.

From 1907 to 1911 the educational researcher, Stevens, carried out an extensive empirical survey of what education for twelve to fourteen year-olds looked like in schools in and around New York. She carried out systematic observations of the daily routines in the classrooms of teachers with good teaching reputations. She noticed

---

[1] D.R. Luke, Champion of Children. Typescript, undated and D.R. Luke, Oasis for Children. Typescript, undated. From around 1950, Luke was Parkhurst's assistant and life companion. She wrote two manuscripts for a biography, primarily based on autobiographical notes written by Parkhurst herself and conversations with Parkhurst. The quotes are taken from the typescript Champion of Children. Luke's material of present in the Dalton Archive of the Dutch Dalton Association (Nederlandse Daltonvereniging) and the Saxion in Deventer.

that 'good' teachers were, on average, speaking for two-thirds of the time (64% of the time, to be precise). In part the lessons were composed of "teacher questioning" aimed at "conducting recitations": the teacher asks questions, and the pupils answer them. More precisely: the teacher fires questions at the pupils, and they respond promptly. On average teachers posed two to three questions per minute (according to Stevens' measurements) and pupils were asked to swiftly and briefly reproduce what they had remembered from lessons or textbooks. The pupils did a lot of the actual work at home: teachers assigned chapters from textbooks as homework; pupils learned the texts or facts by heart at home; the following day the pupils were tested; they closed the books and recited the answers.[2]

The situation in primary education was not much better. In a detailed historical study Hamilton demonstrates how, in American cities, from the sixties of the nineteenth century onwards, frontal class-teaching became common practice. It was primarily "simultaneous instruction": the teacher tells, demonstrates and explains in the presence of the whole class; the pupils listen and look towards the teacher or at the blackboard. The classroom was organized to serve this purpose: benches in rows screwed to the floor, neatly facing in one direction, that of the teacher's desk and the blackboard. The teacher was not speaking the whole time. He often asked a question to which pupils had to answer, often simultaneously. "Group recitation" was customary. "Mindless singsong", is already the verdict of nineteenth century critics.[3]

Such education demands a lot of discipline and patience on the part of the pupils. Because most children and youth were not able to meet this demand easily, teachers were strict and authoritarian: as a rule order was strictly enforced. For the pupils, education was a passive, mechanical, soulless and repressive affair, an ordeal, also in the eyes of critical commentators of that era. Certainly for a pupil like Helen, going to school was a torment. Helen was an intelligent, inventive and precocious child, whereas the level and the pace were tailored to the weaker or slower pupils. Furthermore, the dull and restrictive life at school formed a stark contrast with the adventurous and free life outside the school. In and around the lively frontier-like town Durand (in Wisconsin) there was always something to experience and to do, always something to discover, to figure out and to try out; ideal for a child whose parents were used "to balance well-timed encouragement with wholesome neglect".[4] Helen's parents also offered her a stimulating home environment. Her father was an

---

[2] L. Cuban, How Teachers Taught. New York/London: Teachers College Press, 1993 (Second Edition), 35 and 36.

[3] D. Hamilton, Towards a theory of schooling. London/New York/Philadelphia: The Falmer Press, 1989.

[4] Parkhurst's own words in autobiographical notes, probably dating from the early sixties; quoted by Luke, 1.

innkeeper, merchant and horse-breeder; as a pastime he tamed wild ponies. Helen liked to spend time with him. Her mother demonstrated a passion for art and literature. Helen took example from this. It was no coincidence that she could already read at the age of four.

Going to school was no source of pleasure for Parkhurst. At the age of eighty-three she recalled it mainly as "oppression" and "insufferable boredom".[5] What inspired her to work in education herself? Her own explanation is that, early on in life, she had become convinced that schools could and should be different: already as a small child she wanted to become a teacher and do things better.[6] Whether she embellishes her own life-story as to this point, is difficult to judge. It is, however, plausible that she was intrigued by the teaching profession. From her fifth year onwards she was a regular guest at the annual meeting of the regional Teachers' Institute. Every summer it gathered in Durand for courses and exams. Children from Durand were used as subjects in demonstrations. Owing to her cleverness and precociousness Helen was a marked and welcomed specimen. She was also an inquisitive subject: absorbing everything that happened there with interest. When she was no longer invited as a guinea-pig, she continued to go, out of interest. In the summer of 1904 Helen requested to sit the exams. She was allowed. For the show, the idea was. But she passed with flying colors. This, much to the surprise of the examiners: passing with no experience or teacher-training at all. Not at all surprising, according to Helen herself: "I had memorized all the answers. Each new crop of candidates was indoctrinated with identical precepts. The discussions covered the same ground and the answers never varied".[7] The shortcomings of education were mirrored in the quality of teacher-training and the exams for the teaching-profession.

Reform of a one-teacher school

Parkhurst received her teaching qualifications. She was just seventeen years of age, having only recently finished school; shortly before that summer she had graduated from high school. She was also immediately given the chance to work as a teacher. In a hamlet called Waterville, approximately seven miles from Durand, the one-teacher school had been left with no teacher. Parkhurst felt up to this adventurous challenge. And, an adventure it was: forty-five pupils, aged between six and sixteen, among whom seven boys just about one and a half years younger that she was herself. There, in Waterville, in the latter part of the summer of 1904, Dalton education germinated: not as a response to principles or as the elaboration of certain theories,

---

[5] In a conversation following the celebration of the 50th anniversary of the Dalton School in New York (February 4, 1969). Recorded by Luke, 309.
[6] Parkhurst in Luke, e.g. 9.
[7] Parkhurst in Luke, Résumé, 5.

but in practice, as a response to practical problems: "solving problems as they arose".[8] Four innovations stand out.

Parkhurst had to prevent being obstructed by the older pupils. The best way to achieve this, she decided, would be to allow them to collaborate with her. She asked the oldest boys to be her assistants, each one choosing a subject in which he would be a monitor. Each subject was assigned its own corner in the classroom.

Thanks to the use of assistants, it was easier for pupils to work individually or in small groups and to assist and test them. It was more effective to divide forty pupils among six supervisors than to group forty-six together under one mistress. Such an organization was better suited to the diversity of the group and gave the pupils the opportunity to work at their own pace.

Working at one's own pace meant changing subjects at varying times. Differing subject transitions called for freedom of movement. In order to give the pupils the freedom to move around, Parkhurst had the school-benches unscrewed from the floor. The detached benches could then be rearranged as tables. That made it possible to reorganize the classroom. This was also necessary in order to give each subject its own corner in the classroom: four subjects in the four corners; reading in the middle. The teacher's desk was placed in the adjacent space. That was convenient as an extra space where separate lessons or tests could be held, but also for talks with individual pupils or assistants. Furthermore, her absence gave the assistants in the classroom more self-confidence and authority.

The older boys, who acted as assistants, had to manage their time wisely. In addition to their extra task as a monitor they obviously had their own schoolwork to do. Parkhurst helped and taught these boys to plan their own schoolwork wisely. So many days at school left to go, so much work left to do for this subject, so much for that subject... What do I have to do per month? What per day? When do I do what? And so forth. This is, according to Parkhurst, the origin of the assignments and of budgeting time.

She only stayed in Waterville for a year. In 1905 she went to the Teachers Training College in River Falls (also in Wisconsin) to do a veritable teacher training course. The pupils, the parents and the school board were sorry to see her go. The children and youth were happy at school and the learning achievements had improved. The experiment seemed to have worked. Based on various comments scattered

---

[8] Parkhurst in Luke, Résumé, 7. Continuation of the impression of Parkhurst's work in Waterville is based on Luke's description, taken from the accounts of Parkhurst herself, 18-31.

throughout Parkhurst's biography, it can be concluded that in her first year as a teacher, she has learned three things.

First, when children are given freedom, (a) freedom to move, (b) freedom to plan their own time, (c) freedom to confer with one another in a soft voice and (d) freedom to consult the teacher if they get stuck, then (i) the activity and commitment of the pupils towards and during the work increase, (ii) they are more motivated to work, (iii) they have more pleasure working and (iv) learning results improve.

Freedom, conceived in these ways, therefore leads to more enjoyable and more effective education, not only more effective in terms of performance in domains such as language and arithmetic, but also in different sense: pupils develop "habits of independence in handling their learning tasks"[9]; they learn to carry out learning tasks independently.

Second, she learned that the school environment, the interior arrangement and teaching materials have a decisive impact on learning, both motivation-wise and when it comes to functionality. It is for instance important: (a) not to have rows of school benches screwed to the floor, but instead freestanding furniture which could be arranged to form tables which could accommodate several pupils; (b) to group furniture and materials in corners according to school-subjects; (c) to allow the pupils freedom of movement; (d) to have color and light in the classroom, flowering plants in the windowsills. The interior of the school building should be inviting and decent, a place where children like to be.

Third, the subject matter is not the problem: "It is not so much what as how they are taught which is at fault in our system"[10]. At that time (towards the end of the nineteenth and the beginning of the twentieth century) contemporary education was heavily criticized, but this was usually about subject matter. Traditional school subjects were seen to be out of date and not useful. Educational reform was therefore initially sought in changing the subject matter: connecting to the interests and the life-world of the pupils through developmentally appropriate projects, more practical skills, more vocational skills and the like. Parkhurst had noticed that it is not about the nature of the subject matter, but the way in which teaching and learning take form. Children and young people want to learn, and they can learn, irrespective of subject matter. "Children do like to learn".[11] At least, as long as they don't have to sit still and watch and listen to a teacher who prefers to showcase his own skills and

---

[9] Parkhurst in Luke, 56.
[10] Parkhurst in Luke, 53A.
[11] Parkhurst in Luke, 56.

knowledge. And as long as learning does not entail memorizing everything and then waiting your turn to be tested. When circumstances and materials are appropriate children find "learning as natural as breathing".[12]

The experiment at the Edison School

For Parkhurst, the teacher training course at the Teachers Training College in River Falls turned out to be a disappointment. The teacher training was strongly traditionally orientated with regard to subject content and educational methods. There was nothing for Parkhurst to learn, with one exception: psychology. The psychology courses fulfilled her interest in how children learn and what children experience. The psychology teacher also suggested that she follow summer courses in New York at Columbia University, a university with a renowned Teachers College. Parkhurst graduated after two years and was subsequently bound to the region for two years. The first year she worked at a school in a poor part of Hudson (Wisconsin). During the second year she was appointed regional supervisor for rural schools. In this period, thanks to her work, she was able to broaden her educational experience and, thanks to the summer courses, enrich her theoretical knowledge. She did not, however, have the opportunity to further try out innovative ideas.

In 1909, four years after Waterville, the tide changed. Parkhurst became a teacher at the Edison School in Tacoma (Washington, far North-west of the US). She was appointed a first class and a free rein in her teaching. A notable innovation she introduced almost immediately was folk dancing. In New York, the summer before, she had followed as relaxation, besides an apparently useful course of 'Normal Diagnostics', a recreational course 'Folk dancing with children'. This very course turned out to be of use to her. It would be ideal in the class, she decided. Dance gets children moving; pupils can use up their excess energy. And it is educative as well: learning folk dance steps requires just as much concentration and discipline as arithmetic and learning to read. Folk dancing is educative without being boring.[13]

Although it did not become a lasting feature of Dalton education, folk dancing in Tacoma was certainly a very important factor in the development of the Dalton Plan. Dancing in the class appealed to the school management and to the educational authorities in Tacoma. In the spring of 1910 they asked Parkhurst if she would organize a folk dancing show, with six hundred pupils participating, to add luster to the opening of the Tacoma High school's new stadium. She accepted the challenge and it was a tremendous success. It was such a success, in fact, that after the performance she was asked what she would like more than anything. What she

---

[12] Ibid.
[13] Luke, 46.

would like most, she answered, was to conduct an experiment. Parkhurst recounted her experience in Waterville, a few years earlier. How she had run the one teacher school in an alternative way and what the results had been. What she had learned from the experience: the importance of the freedom to move around, to plan one's own time and to consult one another; the influences of school environment, interior arrangement and materials; that subject content is not the problem. She said that in the meantime, she had given this matter more thought and had come up with several ameliorations. And that she longed for "the chance to put my convictions to the test".[14]

Her story convinced the school management and the educational authorities, and she was given her way, unconditionally. Parkhurst was granted permission to reform the education of five classes at the Edison School: grades four to eight. She was given the assistance of five teachers, each with a pronounced preference for a different subject. These teachers were given their own classrooms, rooms that were allowed to be converted into subject rooms.

The innovation in Tacoma was more thorough than it had been in Waterville. Each subject now had its own teacher: the older pupils as monitors per subject in Waterville, were now real specialist teachers. And every subject now had its own room: the separate corners in the one classroom in Waterville became separate subject rooms in Tacoma. Following Swift[15], Parkhurst was to call the subject rooms "laboratories" from then on. This name was a conscious choice. The laboratories were to be places where pupils are purposefully busy with their work, in other words: familiarizing themselves with the task at hand, experimenting, figuring things out and doing research. A laboratory is not a space where a teacher exhibits his own subject knowledge and tests his pupils by constantly talking and asking questions, but a space where the teacher helps the pupils to do their work well: their work in his subject.

The teachers set assignments based on Parkhurst's directions. That meant two things. They transformed their subject's prescribed learning content into tasks per grade, hence: they translated the work in their subject into learning activities. And then they categorized the learning content in the form of learning tasks into units that could be orderly planned. The assignments were crucial. Their application

---

[14] Parkhurst in Luke, 49, 50. The rest of the characterisation of the Tacoma-experiment has been reconstructed from Luke's descriptions concerning this period of Parkhurst's life, chapter 4 in its totality.

[15] E. J. Swift, Mind in the Making. A Study in Mental Development. New York: Charles Scribner's Sons, 1908.

changed education drastically: learning became the pupil's own work; he could start working independently; he could work at his own pace; he could plan his own work.

The laboratories were intended to provide an ideal environment for working on assignments. They were furnished and equipped to be working spaces, tailored to meet the requirements of specific subjects, with useful and attractive learning materials, instruments, books and reference works close at hand for the pupils and with colorful, instructive or characteristic pictures and figures on the walls and on the windows. In each laboratory five large tables were placed instead of rows of small individual desks; one table for each grade. This would facilitate spontaneous cooperation among pupils working at the same level, on similar tasks. And it would also make whole group instruction possible: when pupils proved unable to work things out among themselves, they could ask the teacher for help; then the teacher only had to pull up a chair and join them at their table.

Like Parkhurst, all five of these teachers had prior teaching experience in a rural setting, in one teacher schools, so they had worked with heterogeneous groups, with pupils of varying ages and educational levels. This was a coincidence, but was very convenient seeing that in their laboratory there would be pupils of different grades working simultaneously. Furthermore, each teacher became the mentor of a 'house'. The pupils of the classes were reshuffled among five 'houses'. They gathered early in the morning as 'houses' to go over the day. Under the supervision of the mentor, they planned their work: what to do for each subject and when? During the 'house' meetings pupils could also help each other to organize their work. What to do and when to do it, given the work to be done? How to divide the time among different subjects, taking into account that the one subject is more difficult than the other, and that you find the one subject unpleasant and the other enjoyable? And so forth.

Behold: "Helen Parkhurst's Laboratory Plan for teaching and learning".[16] The experiment in Tacoma carried out in 1910, and the following years, closely resembles the Dalton Plan tried out by Parkhurst in Dalton, Pittsfield and New York, from 1919 onwards. This later phase of development merely brings refinement and a degree of restoration. In 1912, therefore, the Dalton Plan is practically finished, although not yet known by that name.

---

[16] Luke, 53E. The experiment in Tacoma is a great success, according to those concerned. At least, if we may go by a letter, written fifteen years later, by the director to the Dalton Association in New York. Copy in D. Lager, Helen Parkhurst and the Dalton Plan: The Life and Work of an American Educator. The University of Connecticut (Diss.), 1983, 204.

From Laboratory Plan to Dalton Plan

The most important innovation around 1920 is the use of 'graphs': tables to record progress. In Tacoma, on leaving a certain laboratory, the pupils had to make a note of what they had done for the subject in their own 'subject diary'. That was not really clear enough, making planning their activities difficult and awkward, making them more dependent on teachers and more reliant upon guidance and reprehension than strictly necessary. Graphs are much more convenient, Parkhurst explains in Times Educational Supplement in 1921.[17] In each laboratory, for each grade, there hangs a chart with in the first column, on the left hand side, the names of the pupils listed vertically and in the first row at the top de numbers of the activities horizontally. On the chart in the laboratory the pupil marks which part of the activities he has completed. He is now able to see, at one glance, his progress in the light of what he still has to do; at the same time he is able to compare his progress with that of other pupils. He does not need a teacher to caution, to compliment, to urge him on, or whatever. Besides the 'subject graphs' hanging in the laboratories, other graphs are devised, for instance for individual use. But these all boil down to the same: the charts allow the pupils to follow and compare their own progress.

In addition to innovation, there is also a degree of restoration. The Laboratory Plan of 1910 regrouped the pupils into mixed age 'houses'. The Dalton Plan of around 1920 leaves the class intact, at least to a certain extent: the class (grade, form) can function as a 'house'. The class is also the organizational unit of the 'conferences', class meetings. In the Dalton Plan time is reserved daily for conferences. In Education on the Dalton Plan, for example, Parkhurst warns about the temptation to turn it back into class instruction.[18]

The differences between the Laboratory Plan of 1912 and the Dalton Plan of 1920 are marginal. This indicates that the Dalton Plan, as a practice, had reached completion long before Parkhurst wrote about it in her Times-articles (1921) and in her book (1922). It did not develop from a theory or as a theory; it developed in practice, as a practice, in reaction to her dissatisfaction with the education she had experienced as a pupil and in interplay with the education she practiced and improved as a teacher.

---

[17] H. Parkhurst, Times Educational Supplement, August 6, 1921. Sixth and last part of a series of articles on the Dalton Plan.

[18] H. Parkhurst, Education on the Dalton Plan. New York: E.P. Dutton & Company, 1922 (Fourth Printing: 1926), 159. NB: We use the fourth printing from 1926. The page numbering varies in the different printings. The fourth printing is available online via www.archive.org
(direct link: http://www.archive.org/details/educationondalto00parkiala).

Affirmation, justification and encouragement

The original Dalton education originated in practice and developed from practice. This does not imply that Parkhurst was oblivious to discussions on education or that she had no interest in theory. That would have been strange. In the early decades of the twentieth century a lively discussion raged in America concerning the quality, the content and the purpose of education. The debate formed a platform for advocates of new educational philosophies, developers of new teaching methods and academics with new ideas. Or rather, it was an arena: they argued their approaches in opposition to one another and the adherents to old views, methods and insights.[19] No one in the field of education could really avoid this. Almost everyone held their own opinions and arguments, everyone endorsed and criticized theories. Later in her career Parkhurst is a participant in the debate herself. In the early years, as an eager-to-learn disputant, she must have been very interested.

Initially, she did not take much in, if we are to go by Parkhurst's own account. Up until her teacher training course, and so until 1905, she was completely unaware of what was going on. According to Luke:

> "She had no idea that many thoughtful educators were beginning to question the validity of the treadmill that children were subjected to. Nor did she have a clue that the center of gravity was destined to shift from preordained subject matter to the nature and needs of the child."[20]

Parkhurst was inspired by something different than the example of others: "She was rebelling against her own experience"[21]. Taking her age and environment into consideration, it is not impossible that she, indeed, had no notion of current developments during that earliest period.

Parkhurst was, however, familiar with the essays of the philosopher Ralph Waldo Emerson.[22] She had read them as a teen in 'high school'. Emerson's thoughts on self-reliance readily struck a chord with her.[23] It remains to be seen to what extent and how specifically the Dalton Plan is inspired by Emerson's views.[24] In the Times-articles and Education on the Dalton Plan Emerson is quoted extensively. Emerson's role in Parkhurst's retrospective theoretical justification doesn't necessary say

---

[19] For a good description of the discussion, see: H.M. Kliebard, The struggle for the American Curriculum. New York/London, Routledge Falmer, 2004 (Third Edition).
[20] Luke, Résumé, 6.
[21] Ibid.
[22] American philosopher and poet, 1803-1882; see chapter 3 Emerson.
[23] It is doubtful whether she understood Emerson correctly. See chapter 3 Emerson.
[24] See chapter 3 Emerson.

anything conclusive about Emerson's role in the development of the practice. For the time being, we assume the influence of Emerson's to have been diffuse in nature. Reading Emerson offered Parkhurst encouragement and support as a young adult: it affirmed her feelings and judgments. And it served to strengthen her conviction that education ought to change.

During her teacher training (1905-1907) Parkhurst's world expanded somewhat. Generally speaking, the training at River Falls was very traditionally oriented, but thanks to the psychology teacher she came into contact with academic disciplines. Parkhurst was particularly interested in psychology and anthropology: she wanted to learn as much as possible about what children experience and how they learn. What she heard and read provided theoretical confirmation of her practical experience and knowledge. Illustrative for Parkhurst's view on the relation between theory and practice is something she says about the book Mind in the Making, written by the psychologist Swift in 1910, shortly before she embarked on the Tacoma-experiment.[25] It is the most impressive book she read in the preceding years. She read it on the recommendation of her psychology teacher at River falls. What was it that made such a profound impression? The book articulated ideas, she recounts, which she had already tried out in educational practice.[26] It "articulated ideas". That's all. Along with Emerson, Swift is extensively quoted in 1921 and 1922, respectively in the articles in the Times and in Education on the Dalton Plan. Swift, too, figures in her retrospective justification. According to Parkhurst, reading Swift did not have a noticeable effect on the development of the Dalton Plan as an educational practice.[27] With the exception of the fact that she borrowed the term 'laboratories' from him as the name for the subject rooms, and also that reading Swift affirmed and legitimized her work.

Once her teacher training was over, Parkhurst took annual summer courses in New York at the renowned Teachers College of Columbia University, where influential personages as Dewey and Thorndike were stationed. The summers of 1907, 1908 and 1909 must have vastly expanded her horizon and increased her knowledge. However, a comparison of the experiments of 1904 and that of 1910 onwards, leaves the impression that the summers in New York did not change her educational practice, except for her picking up the idea of folk dancing with the pupils in 1909. The same seems to apply to the summer courses as did to Emerson and Swift:

---

[25] See earlier note and see chapter 5 Swift.
[26] Luke, 49.
[27] In order to test Parkhurst's statement or memory we shall make, in a later chapter, another comparison between Swift's book and the Dalton Plan: chapter 5 Swift.

Parkhurst found affirmation, justification and encouragement for what she already thought and practiced.

The modest impact of science, research and theories might have been a reason for her choice not to pursue further studies. She was eager enough to learn and had indeed seriously considered continuing her studies. She had even sought the advice of two heavyweights: Nicolas M. Butler[28], the president of Columbia University, and John Finley, the president of New York University. An uncle of Parkhurst's had organized these meetings. It was 1910; the Tacoma experiment with the Laboratory Plan was ready to go ahead. The two scholars gave her the same advice: not to pursue further studies at a university, but to carry on experimenting. Reflective practice would make her wiser and more competent than academic studies would.[29] Parkhurst took this advice to heart and did not go resume her studies until the forties, after she had left the Dalton School in New York.

Practical and down-to-earth

Around 1912, along with the experiment in Tacoma, the Dalton Plan, has almost achieved its definitive form. Almost ten years pass before the theoretical elaboration and justification are put on paper. This lack of synchronism between the Dalton Plan as a practice and Dalton Plan in theory explains a certain misconception.

Sometimes Parkhurst's originality is questioned. Certain educational historians and observers believe the Dalton Plan was grafted onto the Montessori Method.[30] Others think it was copied from Carleton W. Washburne's Winnetka Plan or from Preston W. Search's Pueblo Plan.[31] These suspicions of dependence are not surprising given

---

[28] Butler is also the founder of Columbia University, more precisely of the 'Teachers College', the forerunner of the university. As early as the eighties of the nineteenth century, he plays an important part in the reform of American education. Cf.. Kliebard, 17, 112, 113 and 115.

[29] Luke, 51, 52.

[30] For instance M. van Essen & J.D. Imelman, Historische Pedagogiek. Baarn: Intro, 1999, 117; L.C.T. Bigot, P.A. Diels and Ph. Kohnstamm, De toekomst van ons volksonderwijs. Deel 2: Scholen met een losser klasseverband. Amsterdam: Nutsuitgeverij, 1924, 13; G. Geissler, Dalton-Plan, in A. Paetz & U. Pilarczyk (Hg.), Schulen die anders waren. Berlin: Volk und Wissen Verlag, 1990, 12; H. Röhrs, Die progressive Erziehungsbewegung. Verlauf und Auswirkungen der Reformpädagogik in den USA. Hannover: Schroedel Verlag, 1977, 97; H. Besuden, Helen Parkhursts Dalton–Plan in den Vereinigten Staaten. Oldenburg: Sussman (Diss. Köln), 1955, 24. Cf. also: S. Popp, Der Dalton Plan in Theorie und Praxis. Innsbruck/Wien: Studienverlag, 1999 (Zweite Auflage), 63.

[31] For instance H. Besuden, Helen Parkhursts Dalton–Plan in den Vereinigten Staaten. Oldenburg: R. Sussman (Diss. Köln), 1955, 26; C.W. Washburne, Burk's individual system as developed at Winnetka. In G.M. Whipple (Ed.). The Twenty-Fourth Yearbook

Parkhurst's close ties with Maria Montessori and her intensive contacts with Frederic L. Burk. Montessori needs no introduction; Burk perhaps does. He was the founder and president of the San Francisco State Normal School (a teacher training college) and a well-known educational reformer, a prominent advocate of individualization in education. He was a student of Search (Pueblo Plan) and a teacher of Washburne (Winnetka Plan) and he himself founded the Santa Barbara Plan. Now then, Montessori and Burk could only have conceivably influenced Parkhurst's theory, and even this is doubtful; they certainly could not have influenced the Dalton Plan as a practice. This is because Parkhurst only got to know them both after the experiment in Tacoma. Her collaboration with Montessori began in 1914 and the conversations and correspondence with Burk started in 1915.[32]

The relationship with both Montessori and Burk was based upon admiration and interest, in both cases it was a matter of mutual admiration and interest. Parkhurst was deeply impressed by Montessori's understanding of young children, her respect for children's experience, her eye for the quality and the importance of materials and the school interior, and her observant and inquiring attitude. On the other hand, Montessori held Parkhurst in high esteem due to her critical enthusiasm and expertise, but especially because of her sensitivity and responsiveness towards children. It was thanks to Parkhurst's enthusiasm and skill as a teacher that she was honored with the task of demonstrating the Montessori Method at the Panama-Pacific Exposition in San Francisco, for the duration of nearly half a year. It was Parkhurst's sensitivity and responsiveness towards children which made these demonstrations a success; this was also Montessori's opinion. Afterwards she asked Parkhurst to become her representative in America.[33]

During the demonstrations of the Montessori Method in San Francisco, Parkhurst got to know Burk. He came to watch a few times and was amazed by Parkhurst's talent. In a letter written in 1916 he praised her highly:

> "I watched her at the Fair several times and sent members of my faculty to do the same. I have no hesitation in saying she appeared to me the most skillful teacher I had ever observed in my life."[34]

---

of the National Society for the Study of Education. Part II., Adapting Schools to Individual Differences. Bloomington Ill.: NSSE, 1925; Vgl. D. Lager, Helen Parkhurst and the Dalton Plan: The Life and Work of an American Educator. The University of Connecticut (Diss.), 1983, 180-184.

[32] Luke, 54-99; Lager, 1983, 96-108.

[33] Later more on the relationship between Parkhurst and Montessori: chapter 7 Montessori.

[34] Copy of the letter: Lager, 203.

During several months they had lunch together on a weekly basis. Meanwhile, they had embarked on an intensive correspondence with as recurrent themes educational psychology and educational reform. Parkhurst appreciated the opportunity to exchange ideas and to spar with an experienced, expert and widely-read kindred spirit like Burk.[35]

By the way, Montessori and Burk were not the only persons with whom Parkhurst maintained such relationships of mutual admiration and interest. Another is William H. Kilpatrick, a student of Dewey's and the man we associate with "The Project Method", an influential American educational reformer. Kilpatrick had theoretical objections to the Dalton Plan, but was full of praise when it came to the way Parkhurst interacted with the pupils as a teacher.[36] In turn, Parkhurst had great respect for Kilpatrick. She had experienced him for instance during 'summer courses' at Columbia University: "He became a hero of mine because of his ability to get students involved in discussion". Kilpatrick and Parkhurst got along admirably; well into their old age, they helped each other out as friends.[37]

In short: the close relations with Montessori and the intensive contact with Burk do not cast any doubt on the originality of Parkhurst's work. Meanwhile, they draw attention to something else: Parkhurst must have been an exceptionally gifted teacher; a genuine practical talent. She was good with children, as was also to become apparent from her work towards the end of the forties, beginning of the fifties. We are referring to the series of radio and television interviews with children and youth.[38] She was good with children without losing sight of the importance of subject matter and curriculum.

Dalton education was developed as a practice, in practice, by a practical talent. This historical development seems to provide a plausible explanation for the 'down-to-

---

[35] Lager, 103 ff.

[36] W. H. Kilpatrick, An Effort at Appraisal. In G.M. Whipple (Ed.). The Twenty-Fourth Yearbook of the National Society for the Study of Education. Part II. Adapting Schools to Individual Differences. Bloomington Ill.: NSSE, 1925, 279, footnote.

[37] Luke, 246 ff.. Kilpatrick was, for instance, later the director of Parkhurst's small recording company. And in the early sixties he became involved in her contacts with the 'reformed' juvenile criminal Tony. In her name, he conducted an interview with Tony on the relationship between education and juvenile delinquency. Parkhurst was concerned she wouldn't be deemed sufficiently objective, due to her widely known views on education. By the way, why Kilpatrick, of all people, was thought to come across as less biased, remains a mystery to us.

[38] Parkhurst's second career. From 1947 onwards. With i.a. ABC, NBC and WBC. Based on the programs Parkhurst wrote a book entitled: Exploring the Child's World. New York: Appleton-Century-Crofts, 1951.

earth' nature of the Dalton Plan. It has a reputation of being prudent and careful reform. The English educationalist T.P. Nunn recommended the Dalton Plan as specifically suited to realistic and placid educational reformers: "(To those) who would hasten slowly and keep on firm ground, the Dalton Plan offers a path of progress which may safely be taken".[39] This qualification did not come from just anyone: for fourteen years in succession, Nunn had directed the renowned Institute of Education of the University of London.[40]

Parkhurst carried her pragmatism with pride. In her old age, looking back, she mentions that other educational reformers resented this:

> "My colleagues called me 'a dirt farmer' because I dealt with realities. Certainly I had idealistic goals, but I kept my feet on the ground and my head out of the clouds. ... Most of the time".[41]

The down-to-earthiness will have been a principal reason for the sympathy shown towards Parkhurst by H. Bode, philosopher of education at Ohio State University. Bode may be considered the most important educational philosopher of pragmatism, not counting Dewey. He was one of the leading figures of the American reform movement. At the same time he was an astute critic of educational reform practices and theories.[42] He was especially critical of romantic theories of child development and sentimental ideas on the natural goodness and innocence of children. He also criticized the disdain shown towards curriculum and subject matter: the value of traditional school subjects was underestimated by many educational reformers, he thought, while the traditional school subjects have great value for the development of for instance intelligence, the ability to form critical opinions and democratic citizenship.[43] The ideas and attitudes of which Bode disapproved were not characteristics of the Dalton Plan; on the contrary. The fact that Bode held Dalton education in high regard and was on friendly terms with Parkhurst, must have had something to do with this.[44]

---

[39] In the preface to Education on the Dalton Plan, xvii.

[40] From 1922 to 1936. Initially (the tens and twenties) the institute was called London Day Training College; it was started as an institute of teacher training. The Institute of Education was considered at the time, as it is today, the most important establishment for educational research and teacher training in England.

[41] Recorded by Luke, 320.

[42] Kliebard typifies Bode as "one of the major stalwarts" of the movement. Kliebard, 99.

[43] Boyd H. Bode, Modern Educational Theories. New York: Macmillan, 1927 and Progressive education at the cross roads. New York: Macmillan, 1938.

[44] In 1927 Bode came to an agreement with Parkhurst that she would provide a demonstration school at the Ohio State University. This gave the researchers at the

2 The theory of the Dalton Plan

Parkhurst is pragmatic to the core. She developed her Dalton education as a teacher in practice. The Dalton Plan was more or less completed in 1911, 1912; that is to say: practically completed. The theory was to come later. In the early twenties Parkhurst presented the theory of the Dalton Plan. She wrote six articles in the Times Educational Supplement (henceforth TES) and the book Education on the Dalton Plan (henceforth EDP). The series of articles was the first to be published. The book is an expanded and revised version of the articles. Parkhurst did not need much space for theoretical justification. The texts of the articles and the book are primarily descriptions of practical aspects of the Dalton Plan, for instance the 'assignments' and the 'graphs'.[45]

We shall discuss the theory in three ways. In this chapter we shall give an account of the theory based on Parkhurst's own descriptions in EDP and TES. In the subsequent chapters we shall compare Parkhurst's theory with those of authors who, in her own opinion, have influenced her work. From this point of departure, and informed by what we have already learned, we shall characterize the theory of the Dalton Plan once more (chapter 9).

---

university and the teacher training staff the opportunity to see Dalton education in practice. The project was a success: "an epoch-making event", the Ohio-psychologist Goddard enthusiastically wrote afterwards to the deans of the university. The Dalton practical demonstration offered proof for recent scientific psychological findings on learning and children, according to Goddard. (Letter from H.H. Goddard to G.F. Alps, Dean of Education. Extensively quoted in Luke, 129-132.) It obviously did not only go down well with Goddard. Through Bode's intercession, Parkhurst was invited to hold the 'Commencement Address' at the Ohio State University a year later, a notable honour. Especially when it is taken into consideration that this honour was never given to a woman. See the consecutive names of the 'commencement speakers' from 1878 onwards: http://library.osu.edu/sites/archives/resources/commencementspeakers.php.

[45] Of the book EDP part of chapter 1, the whole of chapter 2 and part of chapter 8 deal with theory (in total not even a seventh of the 280 pages); the rest is about practical issues. Of the articles in TES the first three are mostly concerned with theory and the fifth and sixth with practical matters (especially 'assignments' and 'graphs'); half of the fourth article is theoretical and half is practical. In this way it looks as if there is relatively more interest for theory than in the book. However, in TES the fifth and sixth article are considerably longer than the first four articles.

All about efficiency

As an approach to educational reform the Dalton Plan is relatively modest. As far as Parkhurst is concerned, it need be no more than an "efficiency measure": "a simple and economic reorganization of the school".[46] The world does not have to be changed, the child does not have to be saved, existing curricula do not have to be turned upside down, and traditional subjects do not have to be disposed of. The Dalton Plan strives to make customary school learning more efficient. It is all about more efficient education: no more and no less.

Learning to live and learning to work

Efficiency presupposes clarity regarding the goals. What does Parkhurst consider to be the goal of education? Along with many of her contemporaries, she believes the goal of education should be broad in scope. It should culturally and morally form children and youth, helping them to become independent and socially responsible: experienced in, accustomed to, and prepared for life and work. This calls for the acquisition of knowledge and skills considered worthwhile, and the development of various habits and virtues, particularly industry and thoroughness, open-mindedness and independence and a concern for the common good.[47]

Like others, Parkhurst was not confident that early twentieth century education is equal to this task. But, whereas many sought the solution chiefly in revising the subject matter and curriculum, Parkhurst does not believe the real problem lies in the choice of subjects and the subject content. In her opinion the problem has to do with the organization of education. Anyway, there is much to be gained by improving the way education is organized. Any shortcomings pertaining to the curriculum may be compensated through alternative interpersonal relations, personal interactions, didactics, and so forth, in the school. The curriculum doesn't necessarily have to change; organizational educational reform would suffice.

Recapitulating: the Dalton Plan is an "efficiency measure", a reform at an organizational level aimed at making education more effective with an eye to learning to live and learning to work.

Free pupil and social school

Two kinds of reform can decisively boost efficiency: "liberation of the pupil" and "socialization of the school".[48] The pupil should become free and school life should

---

[46] Resp. EDP, 45 ff. and TES, July 9, 1921; TES, July 2, 1921.
[47] On the function of education: EDP, the first part of chapter 1, 1-7.
[48] EDP, 46.

become social. Hence: "freedom" and "interaction of group life" are the two principles of the Dalton Plan; 'principles' in the sense of 'working principles'.[49]

According to Parkhurst, traditional education is ineffective because the teacher is the one who does all the work. It is "ineffective --because the learner does not learn".[50] The Dalton Plan attempts to change this. It "creates conditions which enable ... the learner to learn".[51] The pupil's "freedom" and sociality of the school ("interaction of group life") are the most important conditions. They are the effective principles. How, then, does this work? How do freedom and sociality promote the pupil's learning?

The effectiveness of freedom and sociality has to do with three relations: (1) the relation between freedom and experience, (2) the relation between sociality and freedom and (3) the relation between experience and learning. We shall proceed to explain this, beginning with the last-mentioned: the relation between experience and learning.

Experience

For Parkhurst, learning is practically the same as experience. Real learning is experience. There is nothing more educative than experience: "Experience is the best and indeed the only real teacher".[52] In her theoretical justification of the Dalton Plan, the crucial role of experience in learning is the main theme, both in the TES-articles and in the first two chapters of EDP.

> "It is by experience that we develop and our powers ripen and bear into fruition. Experience tries out the powers, tests the moral fiber, and corrects our practices; it shapes and tempers our thoughts, it makes us tolerant and at the same time versatile. It sharpens our judgment by making us standoff and view things from all angles; it reserves our sympathy without warping our judgment."[53]

Parkhurst consistently illustrates the educative effects of experience with examples of learning to live and learning to work. She makes no secret of where her priorities lie and what she wants and expects from the school. In TES and EDP, for instance, she reserves the necessary space for a quotation by the philosopher, Emerson, there where, filled with admiration, he tells of young city boys, how worldly-wise, dexterous and quick-witted they are, solely through experience.

---

[49] EDP, 18-23; TES, July 23, 1921. Principles as working principles, not as fundamental principles. See further on in this book: chapter 9.
[50] EDP, 150.
[51] EDP, 34.
[52] EDP, 152.
[53] TES, July 9, 1921.

"I like boys, the masters of the playground and the street ... There are no secrets from them, they know everything that befalls in the fire company, the merits of every engine and of every man at the brakes, how to work it, and are swift to try their hand on every part; so, too, the merits of every locomotive on the rails, and will coax the engineers to let them ride with him and pull the handles when it goes into the engine-house. They are there only for fun, and not knowing that they are at school, in the court-house, or the cattle show quite as much and more than they were, an hour ago, in the arithmetic class. They know truth from counterfeit as quick as the chemist does. They detect weakness in your eye and behavior a week before you open your mouth, and have given you the benefit of their opinion quick as a wink. They make no mistakes, have no pedantry, but entire belief in experience."[54]

The school should take an example from this, Parkhurst states: "It is just that experience, individual and social, which the Dalton Laboratory Plan aspires to provide within the school walls." Not by just leaving the pupils to their own devices or by bringing such city pleasures into the school, but by bringing experience into the school. The ways that children and young people learn outside the school, they should also learn inside the school: by experience.

Not preventing pupils from working

The relationship between learning and experience is obvious: experience brings about learning. If we are to promote learning in the school, especially learning to live, work and live socially, we must make provisions for sufficient experience to occur. How then do we provide for enough experience? Well, not by keeping the pupils passive, not by separating them, not by holding them in one place, not by keeping them quiet, not by asking them to learn lessons by heart, not by making them recite what they have learned; of course not.

In traditional education there is not much for children to undertake, not much to sense, little opportunity to move, not much to discover, not much to do, and so forth, hence there is not much for them to experience and consequently little to learn. In TES, Parkhurst compares traditional education to a meal, impeccably served, but which the guest is not allowed to eat:

"Imagine your surprise if someone prepared a meal for you, and then sat down and ate it before your eyes, not with the intent of denying you, but in order to prove to you how good a meal he deemed it and how much it could be enjoyed. You would

---

[54] EDP, 25, 26; TES, July 9, 1921.

be left hungry. Some schools persist in methods which only afford this kind of nourishment."[55]

It is of no use to the pupil if he is unable to experience anything, according to Parkhurst. He doesn't pick anything up, and he is left with no lasting impressions. Further on in TES, this image returns in the course of her explanation of the principles of freedom and sociality:

> "In a certain musical comedy, one scene portrayed a gentleman with several of his friends about to dine. All the friends were of different nationalities. The first course was served, but before they could even taste it the orchestra played the host's national anthem. Everyone stood, but when they were again seated they found the course had been removed. Another anthem was played with the coming of the second course, and in like fashion they were denied four courses. The host was presented with a bill for a meal which had been perfectly served, but which they had not been permitted to enjoy. I beg that this characteristic musical comedy procedure which plays too important a part in our schools, be removed from education."[56]

How are we to improve education? The answer is: by no longer preventing pupils from working. In other words: by no longer denying them experience.

The effectiveness of freedom and sociality

Education can be made better by providing for experience. Then it becomes more educative, with an eye to learning to live and learning to work. And how are we to facilitate such experience? The answer is: by way of the "liberation of the pupil" ("freedom"), and "socialization of the school", thus sociality ("interaction of group life"). The relationship is obvious:

Freedom is having the opportunity to do schoolwork oneself, to organize it oneself (how, where and when) and to do it in one's own time, particularly to be able to work in peace, with commitment and concentration. Now then, doing one's job oneself brings about experience; this means truly oneself, and therefore in one's own way, in one's own time, on one's own initiative and with commitment. Such self-action brings about extra experience. In other words: freedom induces experience and experience induces learning.

Something similar applies to sociality. When pupils are allowed to interact and work together and with teachers, in an unhindered an unconstrained fashion, in variable

---

[55] TES, July 2, 1921.
[56] TES, July 23, 1921.

groups, in various places, with varied means and materials, they come into contact with each other in different ways and at more opportune moments and also in more opportune ways and more opportune moments, the teachers, the subject matter, teaching materials and so forth. That brings about more frequent, more intensive, more varied, more motivated and more effective experiencing, sensing, investigating, perceiving, discussing and trying things out than in the old structure with its rigid order and rules, fixed relations and groups, one-sided and tedious communication, uniformity, social isolation and so forth. Hence, there is more experiencing and consequently more learning.

Freedom and sociality together contribute to education which is truly educative, real learning, thanks to experience. For instance, the following:

> "Children learn, if we would believe it, just as men and women learn, by adjusting means to ends. What does a pupil do when given … responsibility for the performance of such and such work? Instinctively he seeks the best way of achieving it. Then having decided, he proceeds to act upon that decision. Supposing his plan does not seem to fit his purpose, he discards it and tries another. Later on he may find it profitable to consult his fellow students engaged in a similar task. Discussion helps to clarify his ideas and also his plan of procedure. When he comes to the end the finished achievement takes on all the splendor of success. It embodies all he has thought and felt and lived during the time it has taken to complete. This is real experience."[57]

Freedom is the first prerequisite of 'real experience'; in this quote this corresponds to being responsible for the job. The second prerequisite is sociality, in this quote: being allowed to consult others on one's own initiative.

The function of key features of Dalton Education, such as assignments, laboratories and graphs is to make freedom and sociality possible.

The theory summarized in five steps

For the sake of efficiency:
The Dalton Plan is relatively modest. It wants to be an "efficiency measure": "a simple and economic reorganization of the school". The world does not need to be changed, the child does not have to be saved, existing curricula do not have to be turned upside down, and traditional subjects do not have to be abandoned. The Dalton plan strives to make prevailing school learning more efficient. It is all about more efficient education; no more and no less.

---

[57] EDP, 23.

Learning to live and learning to work:
Efficiency presupposes clear goals. What is the aim of education, according to Parkhurst? Education should aim at culturally and morally forming children and youth, in order that they become independent and socially responsible: experienced in, accustomed to and prepared for life and work . This asks for the acquisition of knowledge and skills considered valuable and useful, and for the development of various habits and virtues, especially industry and thoroughness, open-mindedness and independence and concern for the common good.

There is nothing more educative than experience:
How do children learn to live and to work? There is nothing more educative than experience: "Experience is the best and indeed the only real teacher".

Traditional education offers insufficient experience:
How do we provide for the necessary experience at school? Not by keeping pupils passive, not by keeping them apart from their peers, not by holding them in one place, not by keeping them quiet, not by requiring them to learn their lessons off by heart, not by making them recite their lessons.

In traditional education (at the beginning of the twentieth century) there is not much to undertake, not much to sense, little opportunity to move around, not much to discover, not much to do, hence: not much to experience and consequently not much to learn.

Freedom and sociality: providing for experience:
Improving education means: providing for experience. How? The answer is: through the "liberation of the pupil" and "socialization of the school". In other words: through freedom and sociality.

"Freedom": the opportunity to do one's own schoolwork, to organize it oneself (how, where and when) and to do it at one's own pace, and particularly to not be disturbed, to work with commitment and concentration.

Sociality, "interaction of group life" or "co-operation": to interact, work and communicate without hindrance and inhibition, in varying groups, in varying places, with varying means and materials, no stilted relations, not too many rules and not too much hierarchy.

The historical and theoretical context

Parkhurst was not the only one who believed that education ought to change. At the beginning of the twentieth century almost everyone in America shared this opinion. Traditional education, inherited from the nineteenth century, had fallen into disrepute for three reasons:

1. It was thought to be ineffective, because it failed to prepare pupils well enough for live, work and social living;

2. It was thought to show insufficient regard for pupils as children and youths, by failing to be responsive to their developmental levels, their interests, their needs and individual differences;
3. It was thought to underutilize talent, because it fails to draw upon and develop the abilities of all children.

For these three reasons, taken separately and together, contemporary education was seen to be inefficient. There was discussion everywhere on ways to make it more efficient and there were also all manners of reform and experiment. At that time Parkhurst was one of many educational reformers and the Dalton Plan was one of many experiments. How did Parkhurst's theory relate to other critical and innovative theories?

In order to place our image of the Dalton Plan in a broader perspective, in the following chapters we shall compare Parkhurst's theory with other approaches, especially those of which Parkhurst herself reports that they influenced her: these are respectively: the philosopher Emerson, the biologist Conklin, the psychologist Swift, the educational philosopher Dewey and the Italian educational reformer Montessori. Due to her emphasis on the importance of the efficiency of education, we shall also examine how Parkhurst relates to Taylor and Bobbitt, the two American efficiency-ideologists.

3 Emerson

Parkhurst held the nineteenth century American poet and philosopher Ralph Waldo Emerson in high esteem. She considered him her "mentor". In her own words, she had read so much of his work that "I began to sound like him".[58] Perhaps she read him at too young an age, for it seems she did not always understand him correctly. Whatever the case, her approach to educational reform differs from both Emerson's views on reform and his ideas on education.

Critical towards reform

Parkhurst begins her book Education on the Dalton Plan with a curious error. She writes that Emerson (1803-1882) was one of the first to challenge nineteenth century education. According to him, this was unfit because the ideals on which it was based had lost their significance. We learn nothing at school, Emerson was alleged to have claimed.

> "Among American thinkers Emerson was one of the first to realize and to point out that our educational system was a failure because the ideals upon which it had been founded had lost their meaning. 'We are students of words,' he wrote, 'we are shut up in schools and colleges and recitation rooms for ten or fifteen years and come out at last with a bag of wind, a memory of words, and do not know a thing.'"[59]

Parkhurst does not mention the source of the quote, but it comes from a speech delivered by Emerson in 1844: New England Reformers.[60] When we read the text of the lecture, it turns out that the charge "We are students of words ... and do not know a thing" is not something Emerson could possibly have meant himself. On the contrary, he condemns reformers who talk in such a way. The New World in the first half of the nineteenth century is a hive of criticism and reform. Reform movements crop up everywhere, radical criticism and ideas for reform compete with one another, everything is under discussion and prophets tumble over one another. Emerson gives a number of marked examples to depict the trend and atmosphere. In the meantime he pokes fun at those concerned. For instance when he mentions animal protectionists:

---

[58] Luke, 161.
[59] EDP, 1.
[60] Available online, can, for instance, be downloaded at
http://www.emersoncentral.com/newengland.htm. Because this is a lecture and we make use of an online version, we are unable to give corresponding page numbers for the quotes.

"Others attacked the system of agriculture, the use of animal manures in farming; and the tyranny of man over brute nature; these abuses polluted his food. The ox must be taken from the plough, and the horse from the cart ... Even the insect world was to be defended, — that had been too long neglected, and a society for the protection of ground-worms, slugs, and mosquitoes was to be incorporated without delay."

Several pages long, examples are strung together, until after religion, the economy, law and politics have been dealt with, it is the turn of education. Early in the nineteenth century, education was already subject to criticism and there was already a call for educational reform. The complaint was that education was inadequately suited to preparing pupils for life and work. Emerson introduces this as the umpteenth illustration of the criticism-and-reform cacophony:

"The same insatiable criticism may be traced in the efforts for the reform of Education. The popular education has been taxed with a want of truth and nature. It was complained that an education to things was not given. We are students of words: we are shut up in schools and colleges and recitation rooms for ten or fifteen years ..."

We do not learn anything useful at school ... It is the same kind of insatiable criticism and impatient craving for reform as in all the other critiques and reforms, in Emerson's opinion.

Contrary to what Parkhurst writes, Emerson is not one of the first to criticize education. He discusses others' criticisms. And he questions their value, as he does for all reform ideas and practices. That the cited criticism of education is not his own, is quite apparent when we read on. It sounds serious to begin with, but gradually it once more becomes exaggerated and satirical:

"(We) come out at last with a bag of wind, a memory of words, and do not know a thing. We cannot use our hands, or our legs, or our eyes, or our arms. We do not know an edible root in the woods, we cannot tell our course by the stars, nor the hour of the day by the sun. ... We are afraid of a horse, of a cow, of a dog, of a snake, of a spider. ... And it seems as if a man should learn to plant, or to fish, or to hunt, that he might secure his subsistence at all events, and not be painful to his friends and fellow men. The lessons of science should be experimental also. The sight of the planet through a telescope is worth all the course on astronomy: the shock of the electric spark in the elbow, out-values all the theories; the taste of the nitrous oxide, the firing of an artificial volcano, are better than volumes of chemistry."

What do we know by the time we leave school? We know nothing useful. Not even the most elementary and vital things. Ordinary experience is more useful. Just as one learns more by tasting nitrous oxide, than from books packed with chemistry...

The rest of the talk confirms that it is intended to be ironical. Emerson tells of how condescending one speaks of Greek and Latin, the role of classical languages in secondary and tertiary education. He calls it the inquisition against the attention for dead languages: "One of the traits of the new spirit is the inquisition it fixed on our scholastic devotion to the dead languages". Emerson conveys the tenor:

> "Four, or six, or ten years, the pupil is parsing Greek and Latin, and as soon as he leaves the University ... he shuts those books for the last time. Some thousands of young men are graduated at our colleges in this country every year, and the persons who, at forty years, still read Greek, can all be counted on your hand. I never met with ten. Four or five persons I have seen who read Plato. But is not this absurd, that the whole liberal talent of this country should be directed in its best years on studies which lead to nothing?"

It is inconceivable that this was Emerson's personal opinion. In his writings Emerson was very knowledgeable about Plato and other classical thinkers and poets.[61] Furthermore, later on in this same lecture, he reproaches some of his well-read and learned contemporaries that even they question the moral and intellectual educational value of traditional subjects and disciplines, for instance the classical languages.

Here and elsewhere in his work, he breaks a lance for the pedagogical significance of Greek and Latin. He had every reason to do this. In America, at that time, it was beginning to become bon ton to speak with a certain disdain about learning the classical languages. More than half a century after the lecture The New England Reformers this disdain is widespread, in spite of Emerson. A case in point is the complaint of the top industrialist Andrew Carnegie in 1901. We send our boys to school, he grumbles,

> "to waste energies upon obtaining a knowledge of such languages as Greek and Latin, which are of no more practical use to them than Choktaw. ... They have in no sense received instruction. On the contrary, what they have obtained was served to imbue them with false ideas and to give them distaste for practical life".[62]

---

[61] Cf. Plato's essays in his Representative Men from 1850. Available online: http://www.emersoncentral.com/repmen.htm

[62] Quoted in R.E. Callahan, Education and the Cult of Efficiency. Chicago/London: University of Chicago Press, 1962, 9.

The school should equip for 'earning', and not for 'learning', an educational manager wrote in 1909[63]. It is to this kind of voice that Emerson objects; as early as 1844 in fact. He was not one of the first to challenge education, but he was one of the first to challenge the utilitarian criticism of education.

This makes Parkhurst's citation seem even odder. Emerson objects to the kind of educational criticism towards which Parkhurst shows sympathy in her Education on the Dalton Plan and with which she introduces and legitimizes her practice and ideas. The first chapter, which opens with a reference to Emerson, takes the utilitarian argument as a point of departure: traditional education is rightly disputed, Parkhurst states, because it is not of much use to children and youth; it fails to prepare them effectively for life and work.

What is Emerson's objection towards such criticism? He believes the utilitarian educational criticism to be a component of the hype of "criticism and attack on institutions". His objection is a simple but fundamental one. The criticism and reforms are too narrow-minded and parochial, directed towards this or that. What is really wrong and needs to change is not 'this or that', not this one shortcoming and that one ill, but everything, the totality: society, culture, economy, politics, religion as a whole … Real melioration is total and integral melioration. This does not imply that Emerson preaches revolution; on the contrary. According to Emerson, real melioration begins with personal melioration, self-improvement:

> "(S)ociety gains nothing whilst a man, not himself renovated, attempts to renovate things around him: he has become tediously good in some particular, but negligent or narrow in the rest; and hypocrisy and vanity are often the disgusting result."

As opposed to the fashion of reforming 'this or that', Emerson makes a moral and intellectual appeal. He believes that everyone should get the best out of themselves and make the most of themselves, the best in a moral and intellectual sense. "We are all the children of genius, the children of virtue," Emerson says. Let us place our belief in, and heed to this, our calling, and bring each other to account and encourage each other. In this, education has a crucial role to play. In New England Reformers, Emerson already alludes to this: the school should contribute to the development of 'genius' and 'virtue'. Later on, he elaborates on this theme in his lectures on education (On education[64]); we shall return to these shortly.

---

[63] Ibid., 10.

[64] Transcribed as On Education. Emerson held the lecture various times in various different versions. Available online, for instance:

http://www.vcu.edu/engweb/transcendentalism/authors/emerson/essays/education.html.

Emerson was not too keen on reform movements. He expected everything from the self-reform of individuals. This image also emerges from biographical studies of Emerson, such as those by Clayton and by Richardson.[65] In this context, it is noteworthy that Richardson nevertheless interprets the lecture New England Reformers as being mildly critical towards reformers: "wrapping his general approval of reform movements in light irony".[66] Approval wrapped in light irony? The speech seems more like a blatant condemnation of 'reform movements' based on a principled argument, a plain verdict. The text itself leaves little room for doubt. Biographical information on Emerson offers additional proof for the belief that he does not really sympathize with the examples of "criticism and attack on institutions" which he 'ironically' disqualifies. In the list he recites in New England Reformers one movement is conspicuous by its absence: the anti-slavery movement. That is notable, because slavery was a hot issue in the New World at that time (the decades preceding the Civil War). It can be no coincidence that Emerson excludes the anti-slavery movement. The explanation for this is obvious. From the biographies it is clear that this is the only 'reform'-inclination he does take seriously, and towards which he is frankly sympathetic, in which he even becomes involved himself. On the 1st of August 1844, half a year after New England Reformers, Emerson holds a passionate plea during a gathering of 'abolitionists' for the abolition of slavery.[67] Hence, he does not deem all criticism and reform to be dubious.

Improving education

Parkhurst just takes that one ill-chosen sentence with which she begins her book from New England Reformers. She uses Emerson's On Education[68] in a less light-hearted way. Parkhurst borrows an assortment of sentences and passages from the book, two whole pages in all, both in her article series and in her book.[69] To a certain extent she seems to lean towards him. Nevertheless, here too, her interpretation is disputable and her views on education and educational reform differ from those of Emerson. Let us start with Emerson; later on we shall come back to Parkhurst.

---

[65] M.K. Cayton, Emerson's Emergence, Self and Society in the Transformation of New England, 1800-1845. Chapel Hill/London: University of North Carolina Press, 1989; R.D. Richardson Jr. Emerson. The Mind on Fire. Berkeley/Los Angeles/London: University of California Press, 1995.
[66] Richardson, 395.
[67] R. D. Richardson Jr. Emerson. The Mind on Fire. Berkeley/Los Angeles/London: University of California Press, 1995, 395-399.
[68] Available online: http://www.vcu.edu/engweb/transcendentalism/authors/emerson/essays/education.html. Because this is a lecture and we make use of an online version, we are unable to give corresponding page numbers for the quotes.
[69] EDP, 20-22; TES, July 2, 1921.

Emerson thinks we should expect more from education, more than we are accustomed to and that we should make more of education. It is common practice to teach children to become as we are ourselves; while it is quite possible to teach children to make the best of themselves; the 'best' in the moral and the intellectual sense of the word. Why be content with copying if we can do much better?

> "We teach boys to be such men as we are. We do not teach them to aspire to be all they can. We do not give them a training as if we believed in their noble nature. ... We exercise their understandings to the apprehension and comparison of some facts, to a skill in numbers, in words; we aim to make accountants, attorneys, engineers; but not to make able, earnest, great-hearted men. ... The great object of Education ... should be a moral one; to teach self-trust; to inspire the youthful man with an interest in himself; with a curiosity touching his own nature; to acquaint him with the resources of his mind."

Pupils are like us "the children of genius, the children of virtue" and education can help to accomplish this. Of course, it should at the same time provide for the acquisition and development of knowledge and skills; as long as it is in service of personal intellectual and moral development and is not geared towards socialization alone. Education should not aim at children becoming clones of ourselves. It should do justice to the unknown, unique potential children carry within them.

> "Respect the child. Wait and see the new product of Nature. Nature loves analogies, but not repetitions."

Emerson believes that each child is a new promise and each child is equally exceptional, incomparable to all other children, and that, for this reason, education should not be obtrusive and overwhelming, not aimed at normalization and standardization, but modest and varied. The realization of the promise cannot be achieved by coercion; this is in the child's own hands: "he only holds the key to his own secret". Ideally, therefore, education respects the nature and individuality of the child; ideally it takes care not ...

> "(to) sacrifice the genius of the pupil, the unknown possibilities of his nature, to a neat and safe uniformity ... defeat his proper promise and produce the ordinary and the mediocre."

Up to this point, Parkhurst seems, on the whole, to endorse Emerson's view, witness the selection of citations from his On Education in her Education on the Dalton Plan.[70] Respecting children; not being obtrusive and not cloning; allowing children to get the best out of themselves and make the best of themselves; fostering their personal moral and intellectual development ... This all suits Parkhurst very well. At this

---

[70] EDP, 20, 21.

relatively abstract and broad level, Parkhurst could be perceived as being of the same tradition of educational philosophy as Emerson. However, as soon as things become more concrete and practical, Parkhurst goes her own way and little remains of the similarity to Emerson.

Illustrative is the manner in which Parkhurst cites and uses Emerson's sketch of the 'boys'. She quotes a long passage in full:

> "I like boys, the masters of the playground and of the street--boys, who have the same liberal ticket of admission to all shops, factories, armories, town-meetings, caucuses, mobs, target-shootings, as flies have; quite unsuspected, coming in as naturally as the janitor--known to have no money in their pockets, and themselves not suspecting the value of this poverty; putting nobody on his guard, but seeing the inside of the show--hearing all the asides. There are no secrets from them, they know everything that befalls in the fire company, the merits of every engine and of every man at the brakes, how to work it, and are swift to try their hand at every part; so too the merits of every locomotive on the rails, and will coax the engineer to let them ride with him and pull the handles when it goes to the engine-house. They are there only for fun, and not knowing that they are at school, in the court-house, or the cattle-show, quite as much and more than they were, an hour ago, in the arithmetic class. They know truth from counterfeit as quick as the chemist does. They detect weakness in your eye and behavior a week before you open your mouth, and have given you the benefit of their opinion quick as a wink. They make no mistakes, have no pedantry, but entire belief on experience."[71]

Parkhurst reproduces the excerpt, but she gives it her own twist. She concludes: it is this kind of experience that Dalton education wishes to provide at school. The street-boys thank their enviable worldly wisdom, dexterity and self-confidence to their everyday experience of varied and adventurous city life. "It is just that experience … which the Dalton Plan aspires to provide within the school walls."[72] The moral of the story is pedagogical simply: nothing is more educative than experience.

Emerson himself has other plans with the account about the city boys; it leads him to different conclusions. Immediately prior to the cited passage, he writes that, in education, we should do justice to "the genius of the pupil, the unknown possibilities of his nature". Education should respect the nature of the child. "Let us have men," he says, "whose manhood is only the continuation of their boyhood, natural characters still; such are able and fertile for heroic action". The naturalness of the child must be retained; meaning: his "genius", his promise, his unknown possibilities, and the best he

---

[71] EDP, 21, 22.
[72] Ibid., 22.

has in him. Indeed: full of promise, capable of heroic acts. Then follows the account of street-boys: "I like boys, the masters of the playground and of the street ..." Look what they have in them! This is where the emphasis lies. Emerson shows in great detail the 'genius', the promise. Look what children are capable of, without the intervention of education.

Emerson is not finished where Parkhurst stops, when the term 'experience' is mentioned. For him, it is not the about the educativeness of everyday experience and its pedagogical utility. He wishes to show just how full of promise the nature of young people is. And he carries on about this for a couple of pages. His discussion leads to a question: how are we to retain this nature, this 'genius', this promise, while having to impart knowledge and skills and wishing to educate pupils in a moral and intellectual sense? What are we to do...

> "to keep his natural and train off all but that; to keep his naturel, but stop off his uproar, fooling, and horseplay; to keep his nature and arm it with knowledge"?

It is a classical educational question: how do we prevent the necessary disciplining and instruction from suppressing children's potential? Or to put it more loosely: how are we to combine education and development? Emerson is not the first philosopher to ask this question. He is not the last either. And he doesn't have a cut-and-dried answer.

That is to say, he doesn't have a cut-and-dried realistic answer. We must be subtle when we correct and direct, he writes, and we should grant the pupils the space to investigate and reflect. This sounds plausible. But how are we to do that in the school? Not by customary methods, Emerson says: mechanistic and military methods are absolutely wrong. In fact the natural method is ideal:

> "The whole theory of the school is on the nurse's or mother's knee. The child is as hot to learn as the mother is to impart. There is mutual delight. The joy of our childhood in hearing beautiful stories from some skillful aunt who loves to tell them, must be repeated in youth. The boy wishes to learn to skate; to coast, to catch a fish in the brook, to hit a mark with a snowball or a stone; and a boy a little older is just as well pleased to teach him these sciences. Not less delightful is the mutual pleasure of teaching and learning the secret of algebra, or of chemistry, or of good reading and good recitation of poetry or of prose, or of chosen facts in history or in biography."

Well said. In reality, however, schoolchildren are not always eager to learn and it is not always a treat to teach them. Indeed, the reality of the school is a far cry from the ideal. The natural ideal is based on one-on-one teaching, Emerson admits:

"Happy the natural college ... But the moment this is organized, difficulties begin. ... Our modes of education aim ... to do for masses, what must be done reverently, one by one."

Emerson does not mince his words. He is not able to offer concrete advice for institutionalized education, hence for schools: "I confess myself utterly at a loss in suggesting particular reforms in our ways of teaching." The only thing he can and will say is that the teacher should be tactful, patient and wise. Chiefly reserved and expectant: leaving room for development, subtle disciplining:

"Can you not baffle the impatience and passion of the child by your tranquility? Can you not wait for him, as Nature and Providence do? ... He has a secret ... give him time and opportunity. ... Have the self-command you wish to inspire. Your teaching and discipline must have the reserve and taciturnity of Nature. Teach them to hold their tongues by holding your own. Say little; do not snarl; do not chide; but govern by the eye. See what they need, and that the right thing is done."

Emerson does not have educational reform in mind. That would be strange, given his critical views on institutional reforms (see the previous paragraph). In his opinion, the only way to improve education is by addressing the teacher. Emerson appeals to the teacher, with respect to his professional ethos, the ethics of his profession, especially his relation towards the pupils' individuality and potential. Such an appeal obviously remains modest: offering suggestions; we cannot do more, nor do we have to do more. For instance:

"I advise teachers to cherish mother-wit. I assume that you will keep the grammar, reading, writing and arithmetic in order. ... But smuggle in a little contraband wit, fancy, imagination, thought. ... Set this law up, whatever becomes of the rules of the school: they must not whisper, much less talk; but if one of the young people says a wise thing, greet it, and let all the children clap their hands. They shall have no book but schoolbooks in the room; but if one has brought in a Plutarch or Shakespeare or Don Quixote or Goldsmith or any other good book, and understands what he reads, put him at once at the head of the class. ... If a child happens to show that he knows any fact about astronomy, or plants, or birds, or rocks, or history, that interests him and you, hush all the classes and encourage him to tell it so that all may hear. Then you have made your schoolroom like the world. Of course you will insist on modesty in the children, and respect to their teachers, but if the boy stops you in your speech, cries out that you are wrong and sets you right, hug him!"

The nature of the concrete suggestions shows that Emerson indeed did not have school reform in mind. He certainly thinks schools could be better: he argues in favor of more respect for children and youth, with more attention given to their promise, their nature. But for Emerson this is a matter for the teacher.

Parkhurst's approach differs significantly from that of Emerson. Parkhurst renews the 'machinery' of education with an eye to improving efficiency. Emerson appeals to the teacher: the teacher should be doing more justice to the individuality and possibilities of the pupils. Parkhurst's concerns are organizational and pedagogical. Her solution is technical and strategic. Emerson's concerns are educational. His solution is moral; he appeals to the ethos of the teacher and to his tact and wisdom.

Parkhurst was influenced by Emerson's work, but this influence is diffuse. Although there is some common ground, the differences are evident. The similarities are rough, pertaining to: their image of the child, attention to individuality and diversity, faith in development, appreciation of autonomy, and so forth. In this respect, Parkhurst is a child of her time; Emerson, on the other hand, was somewhat ahead of his time.

Besides rough similarities, there are fundamental differences. It is a pity that Parkhurst does not identify the differences or take the trouble to explain why she chooses a different direction, making other choices than Emerson. It would, for instance, have been interesting and perhaps enlightening, to learn her reason for emphasizing the organizational aspects of education instead of the ethos, tact and wisdom of the teacher.

4 Conklin

Children don't just have to be educated culturally and intellectually, but also morally and socially, according to Parkhurst along with many of her contemporaries. It is a common objection to traditional education. That is mainly aimed at cultural and intellectual education, critics complain, while neglecting social and moral education. In her Education on the Dalton Plan, Parkhurst refers to the biologist Edwin Grant Conklin (1859-1952) to enforce this objection. It is questionable whether Parkhurst's appeal to Conklin is justified. And it is puzzling why Parkhurst pays no attention to Conklin's views on education.

Heredity and environment

Parkhurst quotes a few sentences from Conklin's book Heredity and Environment in the Development of Men:

> "Only that environment and training are good which lead to the development of good habits and traits or to the suppression of bad ones. ... In education we are strangely blind as to proper aims and methods. Any education is bad which leads to the formation of habits of idleness, carelessness and failure, instead of habits of industry, thoroughness and success. Any religious or social institution is bad which leads to habits of pious make-believe, insincerity, slavish regard for authority and disregard for evidence, instead of habits of sincerity, open-mindedness and independence."[73]

There you are, this is what education should be aiming at in Parkhurst's opinion: "These are the beacon lights towards which education should tend". When education has different outcomes, it is unfit: "By its works on the pupils we shall know it." Traditional education does not lead to this, and therefore it is no good. It is "bad education". It could be much better. Education would preferably "breed in the young that moral stamina upon which Edwin Conklin sets such price". And that does not have to come at the expense of cultural and intellectual education.[74] Parkhurst makes it seem as if Conklin is in complete agreement with her. However, in doing so she distorts what Conklin writes.

---

[73] Quoted from EDP, 5 taken from E.G. Conklin, Heredity and Environment in the Development of Men. Princeton: Princeton University Press, 1939 (Sixth Edition), 256, 257. (Originally: 1915)

[74] EDP, 5, 6.

Conklin's Heredity and Environment in the Development of Men is an introduction to developmental biology. The author is a professor of biology at Princeton University and as a researcher an international authority in his field. The book is relatively widely read (six editions, eleven printings, between 1915 and 1939 and a number of translations), even though it is quite technical and detailed. It gives a summary of the state of the knowledge in the fields of heredity, the development of plants, animals and human beings; continually referring to examples of scientific research and current theories. After chapters about developmental phenomena and influences, heredity and the cellular basis of heredity and development, follows a chapter on the influence of the environment on development. Parkhurst's quote is taken from last paragraph of this forth chapter. What were the preceding paragraphs about? The first paragraph considers the theoretical discussion on the relationship between hereditary influences and environmental influences. The second paragraph discusses experimental research into this relationship: how, in experiments, it is systematically examined how the development of organisms changes when the environment is modified. The third paragraph deals with the relationship between functional behavior and development. The fourth paragraph is a critique of Lamarck's controversial theory on the inheritance of acquired characteristics. The fifth and last paragraph provides what the chapter title promises: "Applications to human development: euthenics".

Conklin explains that the same applies to humans as does to all other organisms. How a human develops and what he becomes, depends on both hereditary characteristics and the environment. However, the relationship between hereditary influences and environmental influences is different in the case of man to that of other organisms, different to that of any other animal. This is due to two factors: our intelligence and the duration of our immaturity (of maturation, growth and learning). Man is more intelligent than other species and the period of immaturity is exceptionally long in the case of human children. Both factors imply that man is particularly 'plastic': his development is less determined by heredity and is more susceptible to environmental influences than is the case for other organisms and animals. This explains our relatively strong "capacity for training and education". Environmental influences play a decisive role in our development. What would be a favorable environment and what an unfavorable one? Conklin devotes a separate subparagraph to this theme: "Good and bad environment".

We are easily misled, he writes. Circumstances that are bad at first sight can still have favorable outcomes: "disadvantages, hardships, discomforts" can result in "sturdy bodies, good judgments, good morals". Hence, bad circumstances can sometimes provide a good environment. But, for the same token, the outcome could be bad: they can be "too hard, too severe", with disastrous consequences. In that case, they provide a bad environment. Whether a certain environment is good or bad depends on miscellaneous factors, among other things on the inborn characteristics of the individual; it therefore varies from person to person. Whether an environment is good or bad can only be measured for each case by looking at the outcome. "Any environment is bad ... which leads to the development of bad traits of body or mind". This also applies to education and other institutional environments, Conklin explains. This is followed by the sentences quoted by Parkhurst:

> "Any education is bad which leads to the formation of habits of idleness, carelessness and failure, instead of habits of industry, thoroughness and success."[75]

In view of the context, Conklin does not wish to bring forward here that he believes these 'habits' to be so valuable that they need to be promoted by education. He finds them self-evident. He lets them figure in an explanation. He wants the reader to understand what 'bad education' entails from the standpoint of developmental biology. Education is bad when a child fails to learn what we generally have in mind when it comes to education: that the child learns to make an effort and to do his best to achieve something. The same applies to the institutional environments.

> "Any religious or social institution is bad which leads to habits of pious make-believe, insincerity, slavish regard for authority and disregard for evidence, instead of habits of sincerity, open-mindedness and independence."[76]

In this case, Conklin does not so much propagate these specific virtues. He uses accepted American values of his day in order to illustrate his explanation. What kind of environment is beneficial to the development of an individual human being, from the perspective of developmental biology? An environment that is conducive to 'habits' we hold in high esteem. Parkhurst correctly concludes: "By its work on the pupil we shall know it". She insinuates, however, that Conklin stresses the content aspect of the educational objective: the previously mentioned 'habits' -- the "moral stamina upon which Conklin sets such price".[77] Whereas Conklin is using this example in making and illustrating a point: the difference between good and bad education, just as the difference between a good and a bad environment in general, is a matter of the quality of its outcome, the quality of the resulting 'habits'.

The quoted passage on good and bad habits is only an intermediate step in Conklin's explanation concerning "good and bad environment". It is followed by two paragraphs which further emphasize the relative nature of "good" and "bad": "No given environment or training can be good for every individual, not for the same

---

[75] Conklin, 257.
[76] Ibid.
[77] EDP, 5, 6.

individual at every stage of development". No individual is the same as the next. "Every individual is unique and if the best results are to be had he must have unique environment and training, which must be supplied by omniscient intelligence." The best environment is a unique environment, perfectly attuned to individual characteristics and situational factors. This can only be provided if everything is known as to which characteristics and influences, circumstances and effects impact each individual. This calls for omniscient intelligence; which is impossible. We can, however, do our best to improve the developmental conditions of individuals.[78]

Conklin says nothing about the implications of this for education, at least not here in the fourth chapter. Later on, he does say a bit more: at the end of chapter 6, in the concluding paragraphs of the book. But, strangely enough Parkhurst does not react to this.

An alternative to eugenics

What education should do, more than anything else, Conklin writes towards the end of his book, is "(to) train the powers of self discovery and self control".[79] Education should teach the child to get the best out of himself and to apply himself to his work and persevere in this:

> "When education helps an individual to discover his own powers and limitations and shows how to get out of his heredity its largest and best possibilities it will fulfill its real function; when children are taught not merely to know things but particularly to know themselves, not merely how to do things but especially how to compel themselves to do things, they may said to be really educated".[80]

Learning is making the best of oneself. The only way to achieve this is through work, self-discipline and effort: "(it) can only be born in travail".[81] In explanation, Conklin refers to sport:

> "It trains men ... to do their best, subordinate pleasure, appetite, the desire for a good time, to one controlling purpose; it trains them to attempt what may often seem to them impossible, to crash into the line though it may seem a stone wall, to get out of their bodies every ounce of strength and endurance which they

---

[78] Conklin, 257 ff.
[79] Conklin, 342.
[80] Ibid., 349, 345.
[81] Ibid., 342.

possess. Such training makes men acquainted with their powers and teaches courage, confidence and responsibility."[82]

Sport is a clear example. Sport teaches the sportsman to do his best, to endure hardship, to put everything aside with one goal in mind: achievement. Sport teaches him to attempt the impossible, to get everything out of himself. Sport teaches him what he is capable of and where his limitations lie. Sport exercises courage, confidence and responsibility.

In chapter 4 Conklin had reached the conclusion that no one environment is good or bad for everyone in all stages of their development. But apparently there is something to be said in general about what makes an environment a good environment. This is even sufficient for the derivation of an educational philosophy. How can this approach to education be explained? The context points the way. Conklin puts forward his views in the sixth chapter of his book, under the title "Genetics and Ethics". This chapter follows chapter 5, on eugenics, "Control of heredity: Eugenics".

Conklin is critical towards eugenic theories and ideologies, which were popular in those days. At the beginning of the twentieth century it was customary to attribute human characteristics to one's individual nature, one's hereditary baggage. Heredity was seen as determinant for how people were, individuals and groups alike. From this it follows that people's problems were explained in terms of heredity; this applied to personal problems as well as social problems. An example is unemployment and poverty among immigrants from Southern and Eastern Europe in America. That could be no coincidence: people of the same origin in similar destitution. It was concluded that these people are probably defective by nature: due to their inherited characteristics they are less capable, less resourceful, and less industrious. If we are to solve personal and social problems, this should be taken into consideration; perhaps anticipatory measures should be taken: a selective immigration policy is one option; selective birth control, of a more or less obligatory nature, is another. Selective birth control: eugenics.

Eugenics was in fashion. But Conklin believed eugenics to be a misconception. His message is that those with knowledge of heredity and development; those acquainted with developmental biology, the modern research and current theories, know better. What becomes of people, how people are, is not just determined by their genetic baggage. In human development environmental factors have a relatively high impact, as do upbringing and schooling ('education') and one's own efforts ('functional activity'). Personal and social problems cannot be simply attributed to heredity, and

---

[82] Ibid, 342, 343.

eugenics offers no solution. What would be the alternative? This is the subject of chapter 6. In the last paragraphs Conklin brings up the importance of self-knowledge and self-control.

That some categories of people live in poverty, are unemployed, fall behind, fail to climb socially, et cetera, is not necessarily an indication that there is anything wrong with them by nature. It does not necessarily mean that their hereditary baggage is inadequate. It is conceivable that their hereditary possibilities remain hidden and unutilized. Hereditary potential may stay invisible due to inadequate knowledge, and can remain unutilized as a result of insufficient effort; hence the importance of self-knowledge and self-control. The first prevents potential from remaining undiscovered; the second prevents possibilities, once discovered, from remaining unutilized. Conklin believes this to be the primary task of education: that of helping children and youth to discover their possibilities and to make optimal use of these; to stimulate them to make the utmost effort to experience their potential and at the same time to use it. Viewed in this way, education does indeed resemble sport.

Sport serves as an example. In sharp contrast to his high regard for sport, stands his verdict on educational reform: "In spite of innumerable educational reforms the essential reform has not yet been reached; mere refinements of bad methods are not real reforms".[83] Good education, as an alternative to eugenics, does everything in its power to help children and youth to make the best of themselves:

> "Whatever the stimulus required, whether pride or shame, fear or favor, ambition or loyalty, responsibility or necessity, education should utilize each and all of these to teach men self knowledge and self control."[84]

According to Conklin, no reform movement has achieved this so far. His introduction to the Dalton Plan[85] was no reason for him to modify this verdict.[86]

It is curious that Parkhurst does not go into what Conklin writes about the essential function of education, "it's real function", and that she doesn't react to his critique of educational reforms. That's a pity, because then she could have challenged Conklin's views on education and defended her own ideas on educational reform.

---

[83] Ibid., 349.
[84] Ibid. 343.
[85] This is apparent from a letter from Parkhurst to O'Shea, dated 29 November 1922. A copy of the correspondence between Parkhurst and O'Shea is present in the Dalton Archive of the Nederlandse Daltonvereniging and the Saxion in Deventer.
[86] In the years after getting to know the Dalton Plan, Conklin revised his book twice: in 1929 and 1939.

Of traditional, nineteenth century education, it could be rightly maintained that it had little eye for the function Conklin considers essential: 'exhausting' hereditary capacities. Traditional education gave priority to a different function of education: the transmission of knowledge, skills and convictions. This mainly encompassed historically and culturally valued knowledge, skills and convictions. In traditional education, knowledge of one's own developmental potential did not come first and there was certainly no question of exercise in initiating and regulating one's own efforts. Educational reform initiatives, on the other hand, aspired to do the utmost justice to the pupils' developmental possibilities. Parkhurst could have defended Dalton education by arguing and demonstrating that this education actually does fulfill that aspiration, partly through its furtherance of self-knowledge and self-control.

Dalton education does not resemble sport in all respects, perhaps. But the sport-analogy is not well-chosen in every respect either. Conklin's sport metaphor assumes that education has but one single function: that of 'exhausting' hereditary capacities. Although this may well be plausible from the perspective of developmental biology, from an educational perspective it is certainly problematic. Education has more functions, also in Parkhurst's eyes. Among other things and especially: the transmission and acquisition of culturally and socially valued knowledge, skills and convictions. Because education fulfills a number of functions, it is a more complex practice than sport. For this same reason it can never apply to education that it must teach self-knowledge and self-control at any cost –"whatever the stimulus required". Of course, developmental potential should be done justice, self-knowledge and self-control should be promoted, but all this needs to be carefully and professionally integrated into the task of the school, which is to familiarize children with necessary knowledge, skills and convictions.

Why didn't Parkhurst defend Dalton education against Conklin's verdict? She would have had ample arguments at her disposal. Perhaps she had just not read Conklin's last chapters.

It would also have been interesting and perhaps enlightening if Parkhurst had compared Conklin and Emerson. The biologist and the philosopher both believe education should commit itself to developing the natural potential of every child and young person. They do, however, employ the concept of 'nature' in different ways.

Conklin uses it in the biological sense: a person's nature is his hereditary baggage. Emerson uses it in an anthropological or philosophical sense: a person's nature is his identity, his individuality, including his potential. Their respective views on education are even conflicting. Exemplary, according to Conklin, is sport; exemplary, according to Emerson, is 'sitting on mother's knee'. Conklin puts emphasis on intensive activity, Emerson on spontaneous interactivity. Parkhurst could have determined and substantiated her own position in relation to these contrasting ideas: what were her concept of 'nature' and her ideal image of education, compared to those of Conklin and Emerson? Now we are just left with conjectures.

Parkhurst's ideal image of education intersects those of Emerson and Conklin. In the Dalton Plan effort and work are just as elementary as spontaneous interactivity; independent concentration and activity are as crucial as questioning, listening and discussing. As far as 'nature' is concerned, Parkhurst is closer to Conklin than she is to Emerson. Sometimes she is clearly in agreement with Conklin, for instance where she speaks of "the natural talents" education should draw on.[87] However, 'the nature of the child' often means something different to her, also something different than in Emerson's case. In general, Parkhurst uses 'nature' in the psychological sense of the word. When she speaks of "the child's nature" she is referring to "its mental processes and their development".[88] For instance, her assumption that every child has "his own natural rate"[89] of learning should be understood in this way. This is one of the ideas for which she seeks confirmation in Swift's psychology.

---

[87] EDP, 4 and 158; similar to this is her use of the term 'nature' or 'natural', for instance EDP, 28, 136 and 145.

[88] EDP, 71. In the same manner, for instance: EDP, 2 and 160.

[89] EDP, 44.

5 Swift

According to Parkhurst, one book greatly influenced her thinking in the years she was developing the Dalton Plan: Mind in the making. A study in Mental Development by Edgar James Swift (1860-1932) published in 1908. [90] She writes: "I was impressed by the ideas it contained. That book influenced me and my work profoundly. ... (I read) it over and over again".[91] She does not, however, go on to explain what she had learned from the book and she not once refers to Swift in her description and underpinning of the Dalton plan. She does start out by quoting two passages she considers to be key passages. This warrants the conclusion that she held Swift in high regard for his psychological insights and practical suggestions. A comparison of Swift's book as a whole with Parkhurst's theory reveals they have a lot in common.

Swift's Mind in the making is actually a compilation of ten articles. Each article is about development, learning and education, based on psychological research, often of an experimental nature (experimental as in: systematically testing and comparative); it is partly research conducted by Swift himself. The articles combine empirical research, theory development and practical critique. All three kinds of criticism of education, common in America at that time, are recognizable in Swift's work: that education fails to prepare for life and society, that education does not adequately respond to pupils' development, interests and needs and that education allows talent to go to waste, that it fails to develop all pupil's potential.

The book can be read as a scientific psychological underpinning of the complaint that education is not efficient for the three kinds of reasons mentioned. At the same time it is a complaint against the disdain with which academic research is regarded in educational circles. Policy makers, governors and teachers have no appreciation for scientifically accumulated knowledge on development, learning and education: they are uninformed and they do not make use of it. As a consequence, the much needed improvement of educational practice is unnecessarily delayed.

---

[90] E.J. Swift, Mind in The Making. A Study in Mental Development. New York: Charles Scribner's Sons, 1908.
[91] EDP, 10.

Freedom and variation

"Education does not fit for life."[92] For Swift, this speaks for itself. He treats it as the root cause of the alarmingly high secondary school drop-out rate.[93] The problem of education being useless to the majority of young people, Swift believes, is not put right by making changes to the curriculum, for instance broadening it. Many of his contemporaries are firmly convinced that the school will be saved once a number of practical and vocational subjects are included in the curriculum. Swift argues that this is a deceptive solution. The only real remedy to the 'mismatch' between education and adult life and life in society is organizational and pedagogical reform, meaning: attuning the educational form and method to pupils' development, interests, and needs and systematically taking individual differences among pupils into consideration. When education becomes more efficient in these respects, this will also result in less talent going to waste.

Swift demonstrates just how counterproductive traditional education is in handling talent.[94] On the basis of autobiographical and biographical literature, he makes it seem plausible that that great men as Linnaeus, Darwin, Newton, Hegel, Goethe, Emerson, Hume and Wagner failed to do well at school, because they performed poorly, were unable to keep up with the pace, were badly behaved, et cetera. Swift gives tens of examples of famous intellectual and cultural virtuosi, all telling the same story: in education talent easily goes undiscovered and unutilized. We have already seen how Emerson and Conklin called attention to this same problem.[95] Swift attributes this to rigidity and a lack of individual differentiation. "All children are exceptional", whereas at school they are all treated as though they are average and alike, equally average and equally alike.[96] They are all called on to do the same thing at the same time, in the same pace, at the same level and in the same way. Freedom and variation can make things better.

In the autobiographical and biographical literature, there are sufficient signs that point in this direction, says Swift. In this context, he questioned those concerned as to what they thought were the characteristics of the best teachers. The most successful teachers are flexible:

> "The best teacher ... had no rules and no system; or, rather, his rule was to have no rules, and his system was to have no system" ... "The most successful teachers are those whose method grows out of the nature of the children with whom they

---

[92] Ibid., 281.
[93] Swift, chapter 9.
[94] Swift, chapters 1 and 3.
[95] In the chapters on Emerson and Conklin, resp. 3 and 4.
[96] Swift, 31.

are associated, instead of being manufactured in the principal's office, and handed over to the teachers, like any other package of merchandise. Such teachers seem to have no method, so nicely is it adjusted to varying personalities."[97]

Good education is marked by freedom and variation. The best teachers do not uniformly and strictly adhere to a preconceived and preconditioned method, but adapt education 'along the way' to the characteristics of the pupils. This is the only way to do justice to all the possibilities of the pupils. Swift is gloomy regarding the current school practice:

"Uniformity ... arrests mental processes and tends to dullness. ... Conformity to a mean reduces all too common mediocrity. Improvement posits variation and this is just the quality that finds least favor in our schools today."[98]

Swift associates uniformity of method with uniformity of outcome. His concerns about the latter are reminiscent of both Emerson's and Conklin's educational criticism:

"The dominant sin of the schoolmaster is the attempt to make children homogeneous. Nature does not do things in that way; she makes each thing different from everything else, as though to try her power, reveling in the fruit of her creation. The teacher's work is to take Nature's product, and help her complete it... The educator's contribution is to bring Nature's design to the highest attainable perfection, so that the final product may serve the purpose for which its own peculiar characteristics best fitted it."[99]

Making all pupils do the same thing, at the same time, at the same pace, at the same level and in the same way, is anything but efficient and ideal. It is high time for more freedom and variation in education. Parkhurst was already realizing this in practice when she came to read Swift, but she found good arguments in the book, nonetheless.[100]

But, are they really good arguments? ... In the first chapters of the book, the empirical basis of Swift's theories and judgments on the importance of freedom and variation is primarily limited to autobiographical and biographical literature. It is doubtful whether it is justifiable to draw reliable conclusions about education and

---

[97] Ibid., 100, 101.
[98] Ibid., 104, 107.
[99] Ibid., 108.
[100] Although she hardly refers to any of Swift's arguments in her theoretical justification. See later on.

learning in general from the experiences and recollections of individual people. From chapter 4 onwards, Swift is more careful and precise. That is more in line with the strict demands he places on the quality of the knowledge used in educational practice.

Swift is exceedingly critical about the persistent habit within education of holding the everyday experience of teachers in higher esteem than the findings of thorough experimental research. He has a harsh opinion about the supposed authority of experience. An appeal to experience is deceptive; it discourages people from requesting arguments and evidence:

> "Superiority to investigation and experiment ... is making its last stand in the field of education. The chief difficulty in driving it from its present vantage ground is the mystic potency of 'experience'. There is probably no other word that lends itself to juggling with such charming edification and mystification of both the juggler and his audience. It's very utterance with proper unction is by many thought sufficient to subdue any demand for proof of its oracular deliverances."[101]

It is inconsistent that Swift gives a lot of authority to experiences from biographical and autobiographical literature, in the first chapters of his book, while in a later chapter he criticizes others for granting too much authority to teachers' experience. How come the experience of teachers would be relative and fallible, but not the recollected experiences of the virtuosi?[102]

As mentioned earlier: in later chapters (4 to 10) Swift's references and justifications become more precise. They are more academic, selective and critical regarding the sources used. Two chapters are not relevant to ordinary education: they deal with neurological abnormalities and brain disorders in relation to development and learning. However, the remainder is interesting. By way of illustration, we shall now mention four pieces of information inferred by Swift form a variety of scientific studies:

First, knowledge of the structure, maturation and workings of the brain leads one to suspect that two school practices are not at all good for children's cognitive development and learning: a lack of movement (sitting still) and superficial learning (reciting).[103]

---

[101] Swift, 268; see also 243, 244.
[102] Perhaps because the virtuosi are virtuosi and the teachers are teachers? It is improbable that Swift would argue with that. But it is the only conceivable logical objection.
[103] Swift's chapter 7 gives an outline of the state of knowledge on brain development. For the

Second, current insights in the field of developmental biology demonstrate that human behavior is flexible and that man can readily adapt to his environment. This goes to show how important this openness is, given that human circumstances are changeable and ameliorable Education should promote flexibility instead of suppressing it, not only to enable people to cope with change, but also to enable them to live, to work and to improve conditions. In short: "Education should seek to develop a mental plasticity, a capacity for understanding and getting control of new situations, and for making them." Among other things, this means that pupils should be given the opportunity to investigate, to try things out and to experience.[104]

Third, experiments in the field of educational psychology, carried out by Swift himself, indicate that learning processes are discontinuous. He gives an extensive account of his research into learning to juggle, learning to type and learning Russian. The research shows that learning is not a continuous process, not invariable in and over time. In learning processes, competence or insight does not increase gradually, step after step, more and more, in equal proportions, following a steadily upward trend. A learning process is marked by periods of acceleration and deceleration; periods of apparent stagnation or even regression alternate with periods of progression. The course of the learning process is dependent on various influences which may differ from one pupil to the next.[105] Education that does not take this into consideration is inefficient. It is a convincing reason for promoting freedom and variation.

Fourth, systematic research into what pupils are able to do and are able to manage, consistently shows that there are major individual differences among pupils. Swift refers to research carried out by Search, for example in Pueblo, and Morrison in Kansas City. The findings coincide: marked "difference in work-producing capacity" and "great variation in working power".[106] Swift's own research at the United States Military Academy in West Point and the Naval Academy in Annapolis came up with corresponding results: "wide difference in ability".[107] The diversity means that traditional pedagogy is unfit. After all, the one pupil needs more time and attention than the next. Swift agrees with Search and Morrison that is a good idea to individualize education by applying the "laboratory method", independent learning in subject rooms, enabling every pupil to work at his own pace and in his own way.[108]

---

conclusions concerning education, see Swift, 235, 236.
[104] The entire chapter 10 is devoted to this. Quote: Swift, 325.
[105] Swift, chapter 6.
[106] Ibid., 253, 254.
[107] Ibid., 261.
[108] Ibid., 253, 254.

The results of experiments applying this approach are promising, Swift writes:

> "(T)he more able and proficient accomplish considerably more than would be possible with the 'class-recitation' method, while the least capable do not cover so much ground, but, in compensation for this, it is claimed that, as far as they go, they master the subject more thoroughly."[109]

These insights derived by Swift from systematic research and its accompanying theory confirmed Parkhurst's assumptions. It is part of the ratio of her educational reform: (1) not just sitting still and reciting, (2) putting the pupil to work, hence allowing the pupil to try things out, to discover and experience for himself, (3) adapting the time schedule to match the pupil's individual rhythm and (4) taking individual differences into account. Both Parkhurst's theory and her terminology, indeed, seem to have been influenced by Swift and via Swift to some extent also by Search and Morrison.

Ideal education

The resemblance between Swift's opinions and insights and Parkhurst's views and practice is strong. Strangely enough, in the theoretical justification of her Dalton Plan, Parkhurst hardly borrows anything from Swift, at least not explicitly: there is not a single reference to his research and just one theoretical argument. This argument comes from Swift's most practical chapter, "School-mastering education" (chapter 9):

> "The rational method is to work with the students, inspiring them with longing to delve into things for themselves and to make their contribution to the common fund of knowledge, to be discussed or clarified in the recitation. The didactic method belongs to the Middle Ages. It still dominates our schools though, the conditions that made it serviceable have long since passed. Mental expansion of the teachers themselves is the first step towards removing this medieval debris. They will then investigate with their pupils, the schoolroom will become an educational laboratory, and activity will not be limited to the manual training department."[110]

Where Swift writes "They will then investigate with their pupils" Parkhurst puts it as: "They will then investigate their pupils".[111] This might imply a significant

---

[109] Ibid., 254.

[110] Ibid., 300. The quote in EDP is three sentences longer. These are taken from earlier pages of Swift's book. They amount to advising that the teacher be somewhat more modest and reserved.

[111] EDP, 11.

difference (investigating with pupils versus investigating pupils), but a more likely explanation would be that Parkhurst is mistaken or that the difference is due to a typing error, and she really meant the same as Swift.[112] Teachers should work together with the pupils and put the pupils to work by themselves. Instead of a lecturing and questioning teacher, facing pupils who are sitting still and passively listening or reciting lessons, everyone is actively at work. The classroom becomes a workplace, a 'laboratory'.

Incidentally, Parkhurst does indicate that she borrowed the term 'laboratory' from Swift.[113] It is remarkable that she gives such a specific reference, because it was an accepted term in the field of education at the time, at least in secondary education and in the realm of educational reform. In the science-subjects in secondary education a distinction was made between 'recitation' and 'laboratory': the 'recitations' were traditional whole-class lessons; in the 'laboratories' pupils worked on assignments, either individually or as a group.[114] It is probably because educational reformers had begun to use the term in reference to alternative educational methods: learning methods in which activity had taken the place of recitation.[115]

In the last but one chapter, Swift paints an image of what education would look like if the educational practice were to take scientifically generated knowledge to heart. It is worth the while to reproduce this image in its entirety. We shall then be in a position to draw an accurate comparison between Swift's views on education and those of Parkhurst.

> "The teacher ... wins his pupils to their studies through native interests, watches each new nascent impulse to take it at its flood, and so makes the school life one of cooperative activity, in which each pupil plays his part with zest because his individual abilities and impulses are the point from which he starts. His enthusiasm continues keen because he does what his ability permits. Instead of marking time till others may catch up, or hurrying forward beyond his strength, he works naturally to his limit, conscious always of his contribution to the production of the whole. And this, too, would bridge the chasm between school and the world outside, by removing it. Children would be put more upon their own responsibility, seeking and obtaining help when it is needed the time when it is most effective for development. The acquisition of facts whose significance

---

[112] Although the quote in TES contains the same mistake.
[113] EDP, 10.
[114] Cf. L. Cuban, How Teachers Taught. New York/London: Teachers College Press, 1993 (Second Edition), 37.
[115] For instance Dewey, Search, Morrison and Burk.

the children do not see, and many of which have little, would then cease to characterize education. What is learned would be used in what is done, and what is done determined by the stage each has attained in his development, with thought both to his larger racial life and future modern needs. When education is thus rationalized, the personality of children will not be smoothed down to common and uninteresting homogeneity, as the present system of mass education with its mistaken idea of educational economy seems to require. ... (D)emand for discipline will then ... largely disappear in the self-control that experiments have shown springs spontaneously from the growing feeling of individual responsibility. And this feeling of responsibility will come from educators laying aside the lofty pedagogical attitude and substituting that of mutual help, confidence, and fellowship with the student, in place of mastership."[116]

Swift's educational ideal can be reconstructed as a list of ten notions:

1. Ideally, education does not infringe on children's nature, but responds to and supports it.
2. It motivates by appealing to the pupils' natural interests and needs.
3. In this way, school life amounts to living and working together.
4. Every pupil tends to cooperate and enjoys doing so, because his abilities and desires are taken into consideration.
5. No pupil has to endure boredom or has to wait for other pupils, no pupil is required to rush or work beyond his ability; each pupil works at his own pace.
6. Pupils work partially under their own responsibility. They seek help when they need it.
7. They learn nothing unnecessary. Learning takes place by doing. And what is done, corresponds to, on the one hand, development (maturation and what has already been learned) and, on the other, the future (what people need in the way of skills and knowledge).
8. Such education would not turn pupils into a uniform product; it does not homogenize.
9. A sense of responsibility automatically guarantees pupils' self-discipline.
10. Pupils acquire a sense of responsibility once teachers abandon their role of lord and master, and instead put their trust in pupils, assist them and cooperate with them.

Swift's educational ideal resembles that of Parkhurst. The majority of the notions listed are immediately identifiable in the practice of the Dalton Plan: 3, 5, 6, 8, 9 en

---

[116] Swift, 304, 305.

10: living and working together; working at one's own pace and under one's own responsibility; differentiation and variation, also regarding outcome; self-discipline; the teacher no longer lord and master. Parkhurst and Swift were not exceptions. These notions were widely accepted among educational critics and reformers at that time.

The same applies to the notions 1, 2 and 4; these too were popular ideas at the time: ideally education would be responsive to the nature of the child and attuned to pupils' nature, development, capabilities, needs, interests and motivation. Like Swift, Parkhurst doesn't believe this would require a fundamental overhaul of the curriculum: organizational and pedagogical improvements would suffice. Presently we shall see that other educational reformers hold different opinions; this particularly applies to those in the Deweyan tradition.[117]

The seventh notion resembles core ideas found in Dewey and Montessori's work[118]: the choice of subject-matter and the construction of the curriculum are adequate when the educational content ties in with both the development and the future of the children, through which pupils are, in the first place, automatically (in a certain sense: 'naturally') motivated, so therefore do their best of their own accord, and through which, in the second place, what they do is useful by definition. Swift also seems to mean something similar: when the choice of subject matter and the construction of the curriculum are adequate, learning can, for the most part, be left up to the pupils themselves; then they will do what is necessary and nothing superfluous ... Swift leaves questions concerning subject matter and curriculum (what would be adequate for whom and when) aside. He does appreciate that it would be worthwhile to investigate these.[119] Parkhurst is more reserved. According to her, the choice of subject matter and the structure of the curriculum are political issues, not solely as a matter of fact, but also as a matter of principle.[120] And there is scope for improvement in education, without questioning and changing the subject matter and the curriculum. In accomplishing the most essential improvements, the choice of subject matter and the construction of the curriculum are just not relevant.

The difference between Parkhurst and Swift is seemingly minimal. Considering the similarity between their educational views, it is even more striking that Parkhurst barely makes use of Swift's work in her theoretical justification. She only quotes two passages of his. The first of these has already been amply discussed: it concerned the

---

[117] See chapter 6 Dewey.
[118] See chapters 6 and 7 on resp. Dewey and Montessori.
[119] Swift, 262 ff.
[120] EDP, 27.

division of roles between the teacher and the pupil. The second is about the relationship between practice and science.

Science and practice

Swift is far from happy with the state of affairs. It is a shame that there is so little appreciation for academic research, he finds. Schools would function considerably better if teachers were to rely less on their own experience and somewhat more on scientifically approved knowledge.[121] The authority of one's own practical experience stands in the way of sound practical reform. Furthermore, it undermines the elasticity of spirit and the intellectual resilience of teachers: "It is partly because of the tyranny of 'experience', and consequent suppression of the scientific spirit, that teachers have been such easy victims of cheap pedagogical literature."[122] As early as that... Anno 2010, Swift's grumbling in 1908 has a suspiciously topical ring; obiter dictum.

From the part of the book devoted to this subject, Parkhurst quotes a passage. There are two possible interpretations of the quotation and her accompanying comments: either Parkhurst saw her practice as a contribution to the development of scientific knowledge on education (to an 'evidence base', as it is currently called) or else Parkhurst misunderstood Swift.

She quotes Swift where he expresses his regret of there being little experimentation in education:

> "Thus far educational experiments have been too detached and fragmentary. The few who have undertaken them were already burdened with heavy work which occupied most of their day. This left little leisure or energy for working out details or for critical study of the results. In many instances lack of time forced the abandonment of the experiment before its completion. This is the result of the failure to appreciate the importance of the work. Education has been too absorbed in its history. Teachers are constantly straining their eyes by looking over their shoulders at Pestalozzi, Froebel, and Herbart instead of forward to new achievements. As a result, pedagogy is always on the defensive against the charge of vagarious romanticism and practical inadequacy."[123]

---

[121] This is the tenor of chapter 8.
[122] Swift, 270.
[123] Ibid., 272. Quoted: EDP, 11, 12. Incidentally, Parkhurst's quotation shows copy and/or paste errors (or reading errors).

Directly after this, Parkhurst writes that Swift's book had driven her to opt for an educational appointment which would leave her enough time to experiment with reform:

> "It was Edgar Swift's book, ... that made me take the firm resolution to become a free lance in education as soon as I could, with leisure enough to experiment in the search for a new and better way."[124]

From the context of the cited passage, it is apparent that Swift is referring to scientifically orientated experimental research into educational practice. The entire chapter deals with the importance of scientific research and the marginal role it plays in educational practice. The pages directly prior to the passage reiterate the message that it is time for the "application to pedagogy of the scientific method of research and experimentation".[125] The advantage of experimentation in a scientific sense is explained once more:

> "Experiments are of service in education for the same reason as in other branches of knowledge. They force one to face squarely the conditions of the situation under discussion. The relative significance of the various factors that go to make up an experience can only be determined by the process of elimination. Uncontrolled conditions are usually too complex for theoretical analysis. The scientific method simplifies the situation so far as possible, and takes accurate cognizance of the factors involved, so as to separate the essential from the adventitious and to ascertain the part played by each necessary element. Unregulated observation is too greatly influenced by the personal equation to give validity to its judgments. This is particularly true of education, because of the petty annoyances of the schoolroom."[126]

Systematic research produces the best knowledge, according to Swift, but is by no means easy to conduct such experimental educational research. Then comes the passage quoted by Parkhurst.

Does Parkhurst view her work as a contribution to scientifically orientated experimental practical research, or does she misread Swift? It very much seems as if Parkhurst does not fully comprehend the quoted passage. It is clear she regards her educational reform as experimental, but not experimental in the meaning that Swift assigns to the word. Her Dalton Plan has nothing to do with the systematic research aimed at theory development. Parkhurst puts an alternative practice to the test, with an eye to improving the efficiency of education, for that reason only, and not to test

---

[124] EDP, 12.
[125] Swift, 270.
[126] Ibid., 271.

hypotheses. Her experiments are not intended to be contributions to an evidence base, but merely as attempts to improve practice.

Suppose Parkhurst did see her experiment as research and as a contribution to theory development and an evidence base. This would have required her to maintain structural contacts with researchers. On occasion, she does indeed have intensive contacts with educational researchers, for instance with Burk and O'Shea around 1915 and Bode and Goddard around 1927, but these contacts do not revolve around research, for instance designing experiments, interpreting results, identifying new hypotheses or suchlike. They mainly involve interchanging ideas (as in the contacts with Burk and Bode[127]) and 'networking' with an eye to practical gain (as in the contact with O'Shea[128] and again the contact with Burk). Occasionally, educational researchers consider Parkhurst's practice as 'evidence', for instance the psychologist Goddard from Ohio State University[129], but the findings are of a rather casual nature, there having been no involvement in the design and execution of the experiment and in measuring the results. Once, the results of Parkhurst's experiments were examined by independent researchers.[130] In Education on the Dalton Plan, Parkhurst makes a mention of this. At a certain secondary school the relationship between IQ and school performance was measured. No connection was found to the effect of: the higher the IQ, the better the achievements. That is not a good sign of educational quality. More than a year later, after the school had become a Dalton school, there were new measurements carried out...

> "To my great satisfaction the tests revealed that the most intelligent students had, through this method, attained the highest accomplishment worthy of their powers, the lowest accomplishment coinciding with the lowest intelligence quotient."[131]

No more information is provided, not even a source. The manner in which the research is mentioned seems incidental, which proves that it was of relatively minor importance to her. She mentions it when considering the possibility of using tests,

---

[127] See chapter 1 Practical origins.

[128] A copy of the correspondence with O'Shea from February, 1922 to October 1923 is present at the Dalton Archive of the Dutch Dalton Association (Nederlandse Daltonvereniging) and the Saxion in Deventer.

[129] See chapter 1 Practical origins.

[130] Apart from the Eight Years Study in the second half of the Thirties, large scale comparative research was conducted into the yields of various variants of educational reform, among others The Dalton School in New York. Parkhurst's school had been in existence for almost ten years at that time; it was therefore beyond the experimental stage.

[131] EDP, 156, 157.

such as an intelligence test, to determine which pupils are weak and need extra attention.

Parkhurst doesn't maintain structural contacts with scientists with an eye to research and theory development. It is unlikely she views her experimental practice as research. The equation of her work with Swift's "experiments in education" therefore seems inappropriate.

Experimenting, in the sense of systematic comparative research, would certainly have been interesting. Parkhurst might have, for instance, attempted to verify her hypothesis on moral education, an assumption she shares with Swift. They both believe that morality develops of its own accord as long as children and young people are given sufficient opportunity to interact freely with others. Social interaction socializes (teaches and habituates); it is natural moral socialization. Swift expresses it clearly:

> "Morality is a habit long before it is a matter of principle. Because of his greater dependence on the goodwill of his associates, the child, even more than the adult, must accommodate himself to his surrounding; he must adapt himself to the social environment in which he lives. He has not the developed will which will enable him to act independently of his surroundings. We act according to the content of consciousness, and that content in children, inhibitions being to a large extent unformed, is mainly made up of objective social relationships present at the time."[132]

This resembles Parkhurst's justification of "interaction of group life" as a feature of Dalton education. "Interaction of group life" is important as a condition of experience, Parkhurst writes, especially of socially and morally educative experience.[133] Neither Swift nor Parkhurst are able to present empirical evidence to substantiate the idea that morality actually does develop by itself when there is sufficient free interaction. This is something Parkhurst could have researched experimentally. Why not systematically compare a group of pupils, who have been exposed to good Dalton education for a few years, to pupils who have been subjected to a different form of education? Alternatively, why not study the effects on pupils' morality within a Dalton school when the opportunity for free social interaction is varied? This kind of research would of course be laborious and the results would obviously be relative. But that Parkhurst doesn't try anything of the sort, doesn't attempt any research whatsoever, supports our suspicion that she did not view her experiment as a contribution to research and theory development.

---

[132] Swift, 92, 93.
[133] EDP, 19-23.

Parkhurst experiments; in other words: she tries out new education. She primarily bases her reform on insights drawn from her experience as a teacher.[134] And the experiences, to which she refers to show that the reforms work, are the experiences of teachers, pupils and parents.[135] This is precisely the method of educational reform of which Swift is particularly critical.[136]

However much she agrees with Swift when it comes to development, learning and education, she doesn't seem to have fully grasped his thoughts on the relationship between educational practice and educational science and on the relationship between educational experiment and educational research. Whatever the case may be, Parkhurst's experimenting is certainly of a different order than what Swift envisages when he writes about the importance of experimentation.

---

[134] See chapter1 Practical origins.
[135] In EDP and TES Parkhurst, refers in various places elaborately to the positive evaluations of teachers, pupils and parents.
[136] See earlier on in this chapter, paragraph Freedom and variation.

6 Dewey

The philosopher John Dewey (1859-1952) is prominent in the discussion on education at the onset of the twentieth century in America. He is considered to be the philosopher of educational reform. This title does justice to Dewey's authority and influence in the camp of the progressive educators, but easily leads to misunderstandings. Dewey is indeed sympathetic towards educational progressivism; at the same time he is extremely critical of the theories and practices of educational reformers. Many of his texts on education, for instance parts of his books Democracy and Education from 1916 and Experience and Education from 1938, may be read as critical commentaries of progressive education.[137] Dewey has never commented on Dalton Education; at least not specifically; even though his daughter, Evelyn Dewey, was an early advocate of Dalton education. Evelyn Dewey is the author of the book The Dalton Laboratory Plan, an enthusiastic account of Parkhurst's educational practice.[138] It was published in 1922, which was earlier than Parkhurst's own book. As positive as Evelyn was, her father would not have been. Dalton education differed too much from what Dewey believed in and found important.

On the surface, Parkhurst and Dewey seemingly have a lot in common, especially with respect to three topics: the school as a community, learning by experience, and education through activities. Parkhurst also gives the impression that there is a resemblance. On closer examination however, the similarities are not very profound.

In the first paragraph we shall examine Parkhurst's and Dewey's ideas regarding the school as a community. In the second paragraph we shall discuss their views on learning by experience. Subsequently, we shall compare Parkhurst's and Dewey's thoughts on educational content (subject matter and curriculum). In all three paragraphs we shall examine the nature and details of educational activities, that is to say: Parkhurst's assignments and Dewey's occupations.

---

[137] J. Dewey, Democracy and Education, 1916. Edition used: The Middle Works 1899-1924, Volume 9 1916. Edited by J.A. Boydston. Carbondale/Edwardsville: Southern Illinois University Press, 1980; J. Dewey, Experience and Education. Kappa Delta Pi, 1938. Edition used: New York/London: Macmillan Publishing Company, 1963.

[138] E. Dewey, The Dalton Laboratory Plan. New York: E.P. Dutton & Company, 1922.

Democracy and cooperation

Parkhurst refers to Dewey only once. When introducing "the interaction of group life" as her second principle, she states that Dewey had already aptly expressed this idea:

> "There is a passage in Dr. John Dewey's Democracy and Education which admirably defines this idea. 'The object of a democratic education,' he writes, 'is not merely to make an individual an intelligent participator in the life of his immediate group, but to bring the various groups into such constant interaction that no individual, no economic group, could presume to live independently of others'."[139]

The quote is questionable, because it is not a Dewey-quote. The passage does not figure in the aforementioned book, nor does it appear in any of Dewey's other texts.[140] Omitting or changing a word or punctuation mark doesn't help; nor does dividing the passage into constituent parts or combinations of words: the origin of the quote remains a mystery. Perhaps Parkhurst heard Dewey say it somewhere or maybe she is quoting her own or someone else's marginal notes in reading Dewey. It certainly sounds like Dewey. According to Dewey, it is characteristic of a democracy that individuals and groups do not live in isolation.

Dewey's democracy is more than a form of government. Democracy is "a mode of associated living, of conjoint communicated experience".[141] It is living together and sharing experience. But living together and mutual learning is not always democratic to the same degree. Just how democratic, depends on the internal and external dynamics. It is more democratic depending on (a) there being more varied common concerns and interests within the group and (b) there being more varied interactions with other groups. Common concerns and interests bring about mutual commitment, interests and dependence, and give rise to mutual learning, involvement and equality. Interaction with other groups engenders openness and flexibility: variety leads to variation and change through continuous adaptation to constantly altering circumstances.[142]

---

[139] EDP, 19, 20. The same quote in TES, July 2, 1921.

[140] Parkhurst does not refer specifically to a certain page or chapter of the book.

[141] Dewey, Democracy and Education, 93.

[142] Ibid., 92, 93. Some families form an example of democracy: "We find that there are material, intellectual, aesthetic interests in which all participate and that the progress of one member has worth for the experience of other members - it is readily communicable - and that the family is not an isolated whole, but enters intimately into relationships with business groups, with schools, with all the agencies of culture, as well as with other similar

Dewey has an elaborate image of what democracy is. Democratic life is, for instance, not layered into separate groups, classes or ranks; it is open and receptive; it is in a state of constant change. Furthermore, Dewey has pronounced ideas on the relationship between democracy and education. Education can promote democracy, for instance by ensuring "that intellectual opportunities are accessible to all on equable and easy terms" (equal opportunities) and that all children "are educated to personal initiative and adaptability" (being enterprising and flexibility as educational objectives).[143] On the other hand, democracy also benefits education. Both the sharing of experiences and openness are educative and therefore favorable for education.[144] Furthermore: the more democratic our interactions are, the less we are inclined to use force on others; the more we attempt to use persuasion. And persuasion is a "better quality of experience" than force.[145]

Dewey's views on democracy and his ideas on the relationship between democracy and education do not figure in Parkhurst's work. In her theory, she does borrow something from Dewey, as we shall presently learn. This is, however, only indirectly related to his concept of democracy.

It is with the alleged Dewey-quote, that Parkhurst begins her explanation of the principle of 'interaction of group life'. According to Parkhurst, in traditional education pupils readily become "anti-social", because the school is not a real community. There is no "co-operation and interaction"; merely contact.[146] If education is to do better, she writes, the school should provide "social experience", hence "intimate relations" and "interdependence". Dalton education does this. "Interaction of group life" means that the pupil inadvertently functions "as a member of a social community". Through action and by experience he learns to interact with others, to be considerate towards others and to have a sense of responsibility for the whole. It is best that "neither pupil nor teacher can isolate themselves, nor escape their due share in the activities and in the difficulties of others".[147] No one should be allowed to withdraw from others' activities and difficulties. The former authoritarian and disciplined relations within the school effectuate the opposite: "when submitted to the action of arbitrary authority and to immutable rules and regulations, (the child is) incapable of developing a social

---

groups, and that it plays a due part in the political organization and in return receives support from it. In short, there are many interests consciously communicated and shared; and there are varied and free points of contact with other modes of association." (Ibid., 89)

[143] Ibid.
[144] Cf. Dewey, Democracy and Education, chapter 7.
[145] Dewey, Experience and Education, 33, 34.
[146] This, and subsequent citations: EDP, 19 ff. An almost identical passage in TES, July 2, 1921.
[147] Ibid.

consciousness".[148] Dalton education does the reverse and thereby attempts to come close to the ideal: free social interaction in the school offers as much "social experience" as possible.[149]

"Social experience" promotes sociality and education should supply such experience. Parkhurst's outlook superficially coincides with that of Dewey, for instance in his writing about the Laboratory School. The Laboratory School was the experimental school of the University of Chicago. Between 1896 and 1903 Dewey's educational theories were tested at this school, for example the assumption, that children become more social as a result of social experience.[150] One of the aims was:

> "the establishment of the school as a form of community life. It was thought that education could prepare the young for future social life only when the school was itself a cooperative society on a small scale. ... The aim was to deepen and broaden the range of social contact and intercourse, of cooperative living, so that the members of the school would be prepared to make their future social relations worthy and fruitful. ... The aim was ability of individuals to live in cooperative integration with others."[151]

When the school is a small scale society, social interaction and cooperation are deepened and broadened. This prepares young people for dignified and fruitful sociality. In hindsight, Dewey characterized 'his' school as "community-centered" – as to correct the customary expression "child-centered".[152]

Parkhurst and Dewey are roughly in agreement: we learn sociality through social experience; this is reason enough to organize the school as a community, to allow pupils and teachers to really live together and work together. However, the similarity goes no further than this rough level. Parkhurst loosely places social living on a par with working together. She would rather speak of "interaction of group life" than of

---

[148] Ibid.
[149] Ibid.
[150] Cf. J. Dewey, The University School. University (of Chicago) Record, 1, Nov. 1896, 417-419, also in: J.A. Boydston (Ed.), The early works of John Dewey, 1882-1898: Vol. 5 1895-1898: Early Essays (pp. 436-441). Carbondale/Edwardsville: Southern Illinois University Press, 1972; J. Dewey, Plan of Organization of the University Primary School. In: J.A. Boydston (Ed.), The early works of John Dewey, 1882-1898: Vol. 5 1895-1898: Early Essays (pp. 224-243). Carbondale/Edwardsville: Southern Illinois University Press, 1972; J. Dewey, The Theory of the Chicago Experiment. In: K.C. Mayhew & A.C. Edwards, The Dewey School: The Laboratory School of the University of Chicago, 1896-1903. New York/London: D. Appleton Century Company, 1936.
[151] Dewey, The Theory of the Chicago Experiment, 466, 467.
[152] Ibid.

"co-operation".[153] She distinctly prefers the broader concept to the more specific one. Free social interaction within the school supplies the necessary, and also sufficient, social experience. Dewey is more specific. Spontaneous and free interaction does indeed provide educative social experience; however, experience with working together is more educative, at least with a view to democratic living.

According to Dewey, what really matters in education is cooperation, working together: "participation in common activities".[154] Working together gets pupils accustomed to not having to be governed by others, to not having to be externally controlled: not from above and not by their peers either. Through cooperation the work itself regulates their actions:

> "the primary source of social control resides in the very nature of the work done as a social enterprise in which all individuals have an opportunity to contribute and to which all feel a responsibility."[155]

When there is cooperation, the joint work also regulates social interaction: the work ensures that the participants interact adequately and that they attune their actions to one another effectively; the work coerces them to justly consider others, to take one another seriously, to involve one another. Seemingly automatically, the work gives rise to appropriate co-responsibility for the whole and towards one another. Where cooperation is absent, social control (the stipulation and enforcement of rules and standards) comes from above or beyond, or someone is the boss at the expense of others. This applies to traditional education. There is no cooperation, with all the associated consequences:

> "The school was not a group or community held together by participation in common activities. Consequently, the normal, proper conditions of control were lacking. Their absence was made up for, and to a considerable extent had to be made up for, by the direct intervention of the teacher, who, as the saying went, 'kept order'. He kept it because order was in the teacher's keeping, instead of residing in the shared work being done."[156]

Educational reform attempts to remedy this shortcoming. But in doing so, it puts too much faith in the effect of free and spontaneous social interaction. Most children

---

[153] EDP, 19.

[154] We follow the argument and wording found in chapter 4 of Experience and Education. These are representative of Dewey's thinking and way of speaking about cooperation, at least with respect of aspects relevant here.

[155] Dewey, Experience and Education, 55, 56.

[156] Ibid., 55.

are "sociable" by nature, Dewey admits.[157] However, democratic life does not occur automatically and neither does learning to live in this way. It requires more than mere social experience. Schools should provide "common activities". Those are activities:

> "which lend themselves to social organization, an organization in which all individuals have an opportunity to contribute something, and in which the activities in which all participate are the chief carrier of control".[158]

Progressive education falls short in this area. In any case, progressive educators do not invest sufficiently in the preparation of pupil activities, according to Dewey. Preparation is considered unnecessary, as the required learning is believed to occur spontaneously. Or else it is deemed unacceptable, because it is thought to compromise pupils' freedom.[159] This is nonsense, according to Dewey. He doesn't believe in spontaneous learning: "Nothing can be developed from nothing; nothing but the crude can be developed out of the crude".[160] And he makes it sound plausible that well-prepared cooperation would promote and not restrict the pupils' freedom.[161] We shall return to this point in one of the following paragraphs.

Dewey criticizes the 'progressive educators' regarding a further issue. Their concept of cooperation is poorly conceived. He believes them to be wrong concerning the role of the teacher. Most reformers see cooperation as a thing occurring among pupils, with the teacher remaining on the sideline as a coach. Dewey strongly criticizes this "tendency to exclude the teacher from a positive and leading share in the direction of the activities of the community of which he is a member".[162] The teacher should not be on the sideline; he is a participant within the cooperation, a participant with a special status and a special responsibility. Good education happens in cooperation led by the teacher. The teacher is not the boss, as it is working together, but he is the "leader of group activities".[163]

Dewey's criticism regarding the misconception of cooperation doesn't seem to apply to Parkhurst. Like Dewey, when she speaks of cooperation she means teacher-pupil

---

[157] This, and subsequent quotations: Ibid., 56.
[158] Ibid.
[159] Dewey, Experience and Education, 57.
[160] Dewey, The Child and the Curriculum, 18.
[161] Dewey, Experience and Education, chapters 5 and 6.
[162] Dewey, Experience and Education, 58.
[163] Ibid., 59.

cooperation.[164] This similarity, however, brings them no closer together; for Parkhurst turns out to have different ideas about cooperation then Dewey.

For Parkhurst, cooperation has two meanings, first: that it is not the teacher who does all the work, as in traditional education, and second: that pupils are free to seek each other's and the teacher's advice and help.[165] To put it differently: the pupils are active in their learning and the pupils may ask each other and the teacher to work together. This is of a different order than Dewey's cooperation. The basis of Dalton education is individual work. In Dalton education the lion's share of the schoolwork is carried out in the form of individual assignments.[166] Dalton assignments are not common activities; they are not designed and organized with an eye to working together. On the contrary. Assignments translate the subject matter into chunks of individual work. Working with assignments ensures that the pupil regards and carries out the schoolwork as his own work, as his job. It is work carried out independently. He can and may consult other pupils, confer with others, seek help and advice from the teacher, but it remains his own work.

With regard to form and/or content, Dalton assignments do not enforce cooperation. The manner in which the assignments are organized, for instance the use of contracts and keeping track of progress and results (with the aid of graphs), is consistently geared towards individual work. Cooperativeness in Dalton education has to do with the entourage of working on assignments: the social interaction within the school. There is a good reason why Parkhurst makes a distinction between, on the one hand, "the way in which the child lives, while doing his work, the way in which he functions as a member of society" and "what he does or the particular method he … employ(s)", on the other hand.[167] Ideally, the first is socially educative; the second is not necessarily so:

> "It is the social experience attendant to the tasks, not the tasks or acts in themselves, which occasion and further growth."[168]

Dalton assignments do not induce cooperation. In a sense, the assignment is meant to lead to less cooperation. Working with assignments implies that the pupil is able to do a relatively large proportion of the work on his own, without dependence on the instructing teacher. The teacher chooses the assignment or composes the assignment, the teacher assigns the task, introduces the task, supervises progress and

---

[164] EDP, 10 and 22, 23. Also Swift. Cf. Swift, 300.
[165] Ibid.
[166] EDP, especially chapter 5; TES, July 30, 1921.
[167] TES, July 9, 1921.
[168] Ibid.

judges results, but the assignment itself is the pupil's own work. That is radically different to what Dewey had in mind.

Whereas Dewey regards education as cooperation by definition and sees the majority of activities as common activities, Parkhurst views education chiefly as working independently, cooperating with others when necessary.

Experience and education

The school as a community does not mean the same to Parkhurst as it does to Dewey. There are also fundamental differences in other areas, notwithstanding similar phraseology. The second point of difference concerns learning by experience. For Parkhurst this is a simple psychological notion: people learn by trying things out. And a general notion: people become more skilled, more sensible and wiser through experience. Dewey employs a more precise and well thought-out concept of experience: experiences have to meet certain requirements in order to be educational meaningful and valuable.

Dewey believes, along with Parkhurst, and the majority of progressive educators, that "all genuine education comes about through experience".[169] He warns, however, that education is not the same as experience. All experience brings about learning, but not every experience is "educative" and some experiences are "mis-educative".[170] Which experiences are educative and which are mis-educative? According to Dewey, two normative principles are relevant here. The first principle has to do with consequences, the second with culture and context. First: an experience is educative if it broadens and enriches the possibilities for future experience. Second: an experience is educative if it opens up and utilizes others' experiences. Dewey calls the first "continuity" and the second "interaction".

Continuity: an experience is educationally meaningful and valuable when it is a step up to new experiences, when it opens up more experiences, making further experiences possible, which are in turn pedagogically and didactically meaningful and valuable. When an experience brings about the opposite, it is mis-educative, for instance when it restricts sensitivity and receptiveness, when it leads to short-sightedness and unsociability, when it produces blind habits and taking things for granted, when it gives way to indifference.

> "Any experience is mis-educative that has the effect of arresting or distorting the growth of further experience. An experience may be such as to engender callousness; it may produce lack of sensitivity and of responsiveness. Then the

---

[169] Dewey, Experience and Education, 25.
[170] Ibid.

possibilities of having richer experience in the future are restricted. Again, a given experience may increase a person's automatic skill in a particular direction and yet tend to land him in a groove or rut; the effect again is to narrow the field of further experience. An experience may be immediately enjoyable and yet promote the formation of a slack and careless attitude; this attitude then operates to modify the quality of subsequent experiences so as to prevent a person from getting out of them what they have to give."[171]

Interaction: an experience is educationally meaningful and valuable if it opens up and incorporates others' experiences. When it accesses and uses others' experiences. In other words: when it opens up and engages what others have already experienced and learned, invented and discovered, thought and conceived, designed and produced. Experiences are educative when they familiarize the child with culture and context: tradition and civilization, science and technology, knowledge and skills, instruments and tools, means and procedures. An experience is mis-educative when it doesn't go much further than the child's inner experience and what he believes and wants, when it sticks too close to the child's personal perceptions, interests and motives,[172] and when it fails to contribute to the enrichment and organization of knowledge and ideas:

> "No experience is educative that does not tend to knowledge of more facts and entertaining of more ideas and to a better, more orderly, arrangement of them."[173]

Continuity and interaction together form the measure of the educational significance and value of experiences.[174] Education should provide experiences that expand the child's experiential possibilities and simultaneously familiarize the child with knowledge, skills, technology and other aspects of the cultural context. Traditional education did nothing with and through experience: children learned "from text and teachers", not "through experience".[175] Educational reform initiatives, on the other hand, rely entirely upon learning through experience. But they are not critical enough, as far as Dewey is concerned, when it comes to the quality of that experience:

---

[171] Ibid., 25, 26.
[172] Ibid., 39-45.
[173] Ibid., 82.
[174] Ibid., 44, 45.
[175] Ibid., 19.

"It is not enough to insist upon the necessity of experience, nor even of activity in experience. Everything depends upon the quality of the experience which is had."[176]

Dewey urges educational reformers to do more to change this. The principle of continuity (or: "experiential continuum") means that "present experiences that live fruitfully and creatively in subsequent experiences" should be systematically provided. Organizing the entire educational process in order to achieve this, demands inventive and expert planning and organization: an appropriate and consistent way of "deciding upon subject matter, upon matters of instruction and discipline, and upon material equipment and social organization of the school".[177] There is nothing improvisatory about this. The second principle adds to the complexity. The principle of interaction entails that this organization and design has to make systematic provisions for linking the cultural context to the development of children's capabilities, experience and interest. This is broader in scope than simply following the child, being 'child-centered', 'Vom Kinde Aus' or 'learner-directed'.

This requires an exacting approach. Whether certain work, with regard to certain subject matter, to be carried out by the teacher together with certain pupils, offers appropriate and necessary and furthermore educative experience depends on a number of factors. It depends on the nature and the characteristics of the subject matter and on the circumstances and characteristics of the pupils.[178] This calls for expert and well-thought-out preparation. It would not be possible without a made-to-measure and well-constructed curriculum. We shall return to this in the next paragraph.

Contrary to Dewey, Parkhurst is content with a simple psychological concept of experience in combination with a general notion of experience: we learn by trying out and we become more proficient, more sensible and wiser through experience. An example of the latter:

"Experience is valuable. It is the experienced man in any given work or profession who is in demand, and who is held at a premium. It is by experience that we develop and that our powers ripen and bear into fruition. Experience tries out the powers, tests the moral fibre, and corrects our practices; it shapes and tempers our thoughts, it makes us tolerant and at the same time versatile."[179]

---

[176] Ibid., 27.
[177] Ibid., 28.
[178] Dewey, Experience and Education, chapters 2, 3 and 4.
[179] TES, July 9, 1921.

We came across an example of Parkhurst's psychological concept there where she discusses the educative nature of social experience: we try out social interaction; through this we automatically perceive how others react to us, what others expect, what is accepted and what not, what is appreciated and what not, how dependent we are of others and how dependent they are of us, what the rules and regularities of all this are.[180] The same notion is reflected in Parkhurst's account of the benefits of assignments as the pupil's own work:

> "Children learn, if we would only believe it, just as men and women learn, by adjusting means to ends. What does a pupil do when given, as he is given by the Dalton Laboratory Plan, responsibility for the performance of such and such work? Instinctively he seeks the best way of achieving it. Then having decided, he proceeds to act upon that decision. Supposing his plan does not seem to fit his purpose, he discards it and tries another."[181]

Learning through experience is a less precise principle than it is in Dewey's case. The fact that Parkhurst does not pay attention to the importance of (what Dewey calls) continuity and interaction is not readily noticeable due to her focus on comprehensive skills. When she discusses the how, the what and the why of learning through experience, she means learning to live, learning to work, learning to live and work together, learning to plan, learning to learn: general or comprehensive skills, never specific subject matter. The skills are so vaguely fleshed out and outlined, that the significance and the problem of continuity and interaction are not obvious. There doesn't seem to be a curriculum required.

Take learning to work. According to Parkhurst this is an important function of education. The school should help children to learn how to work.[182] It is learning through experience:

> "By permitting them real jobs sufficient to challenge their mental powers, and to realize that even if their responsibilities are carried awkwardly in the beginning, later, with experience, they are dispatched with ease."[183]

Children learn how to work by allowing them to tackle real jobs. This may not go smoothly at first, but, through experience, the children will improve. When described in this way, learning to work through working would seem to proceed automatically: spontaneously and autonomously. However, this characterization distorts reality, as on closer examination this process does not proceed automatically;

---

[180] EDP, 18-23. Also TES, July 2, 1921.
[181] EDP, 23.
[182] TES, July 30, 1921.
[183] Ibid.

not according to Parkhurst either. It is a prerequisite that pupils experience the work as challenging, she writes: they have to be real jobs, "sufficient to challenge their mental powers".[184] The work should be linked to what pupils find interesting. Elsewhere, Parkhurst mentions another condition: "The job must be determined by the limitations of his experience".[185] The work should match pupils' abilities. In other words: Parkhurst recognizes that work is not educative per se, with an eye to learning to work; motivation and competence place demands on the work, on its content and level. This presupposes a certain content and sequence of activities. Apparently, and this is also Parkhurst's belief, children do not automatically learn to work through working; they learn to work by following a certain program. Evidently, in order to learn such a comprehensive skill through experience, a curriculum is necessary. This means that continuity and interaction are indeed relevant.

In summary: as opposed to Dewey, Parkhurst pays no attention to the importance of continuity and interaction in her writings on the subject of learning by experience. A possible explanation is her focus on general and comprehensive skills. This does not, however, provide sufficient justification, because learning such skills through experience also requires programming in which continuity and interaction are important and problematic. If Parkhurst had explicitly linked learning through experience to specific learning content, it would have been more difficult for her to ignore or overlook the significance of continuity and interaction. In that case it would not have been so easy for her to choose to ignore the curriculum and to leave it as it is. This brings us to a third difference between Parkhurst and Dewey.

Subject matter and the curriculum

The debate on education in America at the beginning of the twentieth century was mainly about content: subject matter, school subjects and the curriculum. "The struggle for the American curriculum," historians call it.[186] Advocates of the traditional subjects were opposed to various kinds of reformers who all held their particular views on what children and young people should learn at school. Dewey and Parkhurst both occupy exceptional positions in this discussion. Parkhurst tries to not become involved in the discussion and Dewey attempts to transcend it.

---

[184] Ibid.
[185] TES, July 16, 1921.
[186] See H.M. Kliebard, The Struggle for the American Currciculum. New York/London: Routledge Falmer, 2004.

The education historian Kliebard distinguishes four parties in the struggle for the American curriculum, each with a different idea of what should determine the choice of subject matter and the construction of the curriculum.[187]

1. Cultural transmission. The defenders of the traditional curriculum viewed cultural transmission as the main function of the school. The subjects represent the attainments of Western civilization. The new generation has to be brought into contact with this heritage, for guidance and in order to reap its fruits, but also to in turn modify it, to develop civilization further.

2. The development of the child. A sizeable and important category of reformers felt that educational content should correspond to the pupils' development, the development of their needs, interests and capabilities. Ideally, the curriculum would be attuned to the concerns, the interests and the maturation of pupils in each new developmental stage.

3. Social efficiency. Another equally large and important category of reformers considered it the objective of the school to instill children with the knowledge and skills needed later on to manage as adults, to lead a decent life, to have an occupation, and to make themselves useful in other ways.

4. Social melioration. Some reformers believed that the school should not prepare children and young people for an adult life in the world as it is. The school should play a key role in improving that world. Education can be used to combat injustice and inequality, abuse of power and criminality.

When it came to educational reform, everyone's initial thoughts were about improving the subject matter and the curriculum. But Parkhurst saw this differently. Improvement of education is possible without changing the content, she believed. The Dalton Plan is "a simple and economic reorganization of the school ... It does not add to or change the curriculum".[188] She refused to become involved in the discussion of the choice of subject matter: "I refrain from dogmatizing on what subjects should be included in the curriculum".[189] The problem is not the content, according to Parkhurst:

---

[187] Kliebard respectively calls them: "humanists", "develop mentalists", "social efficiency educators" and "social meliorists". Kliebard, 23-25.
[188] TES, July 2, 1921.
[189] EDP, 27.

"Just what shall be put in or left out of school curricula will be a matter of debate until the educational world awakens to the fact that the curriculum is not the chief problem".[190]

The real problems have to do with working methods and division of tasks, the organization of schoolwork and the relations within the school. Those are the aspects the Dalton Plan wants to tackle. It is an improvement of education which would suit every school, irrespective of subject matter and curriculum. Not becoming involved in the discussion on curriculum may have been attractive with an eye to the dissemination of her ideas, but whether it was wise from the perspective of content, remains to be seen. Whatever be the case: Parkhurst's attitude differs significantly to that of Dewey.

Dewey did take part in the discussion on the curriculum.[191] He does not adhere to any one of the four parties mentioned earlier, but was critical of the discussion, initially especially the contributions of the first two parties, later on also that of the third —the fourth party only came into the picture after 1930. Dewey was particularly critical of the distortion caused by mutual caricatures and the practical bias and one-sidedness this gives rise to. The function of education is not either cultural transmission or the development of the child or social efficiency. In Dewey's opinion education has all three functions. Furthermore, none of these functions is conceivable or fulfill able without the others. The real art is to organize education accordingly. Illustrative for Dewey's line of reasoning and his way of thinking is his argumentation in The Child and the Curriculum from 1902.

In this book Dewey defines education as a process which interrelates two factors:

> "The fundamental factors in the educative process are an immature, undeveloped being; and certain social aims, meanings, values incarnate in the matured experience of the adult. The educative process is the due interaction of these forces."[192]

---

[190] TES, July 9, 1921.

[191] As early as the nineties of the nineteenth century, and forty years later, in the thirties of the twentieth century, still. For instance in: Interest as related to will from 1896, Interpretation of the Culture-Epoch-Theory from 1896, The psychological aspect of the School Curriculum from 1897, The School and Society from 1899, The Child and the Curriculum from 1902, Democracy and Education from 1916 and Experience and Education from 1938.

[192] J. Dewey, The Child and the Curriculum. Chicago/London: The University of Chicago Press, 1902, 4.

Education is the interaction between the undeveloped experience of the child and the further developed experience of the adult world.[193] The discussion on the curriculum distorts the process. In the discussion the two factors are conceived in stark contrast to each other: the child versus the curriculum, "individual nature versus social culture".[194] In doing so, the overlap and the interaction between the two factors are overlooked.

The tendency to form contrasts is understandable. The child's experience and the traditional curriculum do indeed seem like two separate, incongruous worlds: the immediate, intimate and personal world of the child is very different to the wide, distant and impersonal world of the subject matter; the coherent and unambiguous world of the child differs strongly from the specialized and divided up world of the subject matter; the practical and emotional relations in the world of the child differ considerably from the abstract logical arrangements in the world of the subject matter.

> "(F)irst, the narrow but personal world of the child against the impersonal but infinitely extended world of space and time; second, the unity, the single wholeheartedness of the child's life, and the specializations and divisions of the curriculum; third, an abstract principle of logical classification and arrangement, and the practical and emotional bonds of child life."[195]

But the differences between the two worlds are made absolute, both by the defenders of the traditional curriculum and the educational reformers.[196] The two parties are equally one-sided in their thinking. The reformers demonstrate a one-sided and exclusive appreciation of the child's world of immediacy, intimacy, individuality, unambiguousness, concreteness and emotion. The traditionalists demonstrate an equally one-sided and exclusive appreciation for the realm of the subject-matter, with its emphasis on competence, pragmatism, organization, clarity and objectivity. The reformers believe that education should be about growth and self-realization. The traditionalists, in turn, believe that education should impart knowledge, insight and skills. The reformers focus on learning: the child's own activity, preferably from his own perspective, based on his own initiative, his own interest; in this case subject matter is food for the mind. The traditionalists focus on teaching: the activity of the teacher, for the benefit of the pupils, but determined by the subject matter,

---

[193] Hence the term 'interaction' as a name for one of the criteria of 'educative' experience. See the previous paragraph.
[194] Ibid., 5.
[195] Ibid., 7.
[196] Dewey has reformers in mind who place much emphasis on child development, Kliebard's "develop mentalists". The defenders of the traditional curriculum are of course Kliebard's "humanists".

corresponding, as regards content and structure, to a certain subject (a domain of knowledge and competence such as language, arithmetic and mathematics, physics or history).[197] These dichotomies evoke other contrasts, for instance: interest and motivation versus discipline, freedom versus control, spontaneity versus rules, and the friendly teacher who is competent with children versus the teacher-scholar who is an expert in terms of subject matter.[198]

Although forming contrasts may be understandable; it is neither wise nor fertile. The contrasts are theoretically constructed abstractions. They don't make the practice more insightful and they certainly don't lead to an improved practice. Dewey points to the correspondence and the continuity between the world of the child and the world of the subject matter. There are not only differences. The child's experience does not necessarily have to be set in opposition to the subject matter. An important likeness is that subject matter is really experience too:

> "(T)he various studies, arithmetic, geography, language, botany, etc., are themselves experience –they are that of the race. They embody the cumulative outcome of the efforts, the strivings, and the successes of the human race generation after generation. They present this, not as a mere accumulation, not as a miscellaneous heap of separate bits of experience, but in some organized and systematized way that is, as reflectively formulated."[199]

The knowledge and skills which constitute the subject matter have developed in the course of human history as a response to practical problems and have proved their usefulness in connection with those practical problems. In this development, the main driving and guiding forces have to do with fulfilling the necessities of life and preventing or remedying social problems, hence activities such as: nourishing, building, clothing, trading, warming, managing, protecting, distributing and governing.

The curriculum represents accumulated and solidified experience, which, throughout the generations, has been amassed and increased, broadened and refined. Education presents it in a polished, fixed and structured form, but it is still experience. The child's experience is undeveloped; the subject matter represents matured experience. From this perspective education is the process in which the child's experience matures, in which experience expands, improves, deepens and becomes more objective, approaching matured experience. Viewed in this way "the child and the

---

[197] Dewey, The Child and the Curriculum, 7-9.
[198] Ibid., 10.
[199] Ibid., 12.

curriculum are simply two limits which define a single process", a process characterized by:

> "continuous reconstruction, moving from the child's present experience out into that represented by the organized bodies of truth that we call studies".[200]

Traditional education falls short because it attempts to replace the pupils experience instead of reconstructing it. Educational reform falls short because it shows too much respect for the children's own experience.

What does education, viewed as an effective reconstruction of experience, look like? Dewey's answer boils down to the following. What we should not be doing, is overappreciating and sparing the pupils' immediate experience – the mistake often made in educational reform. We should also not be doing the opposite: presenting more matured experience to pupils, or imposing it upon them, as a ready-made alternative to their own experiences, as in traditional education. The aim is that the pupils' experience develops, that pupils follow and experience themselves the cultural-historical maturation. We have already established that the knowledge and skill, which are to be made one's own, have developed in the course of history as answers to practical problems and that they have proved their usefulness in relation to these problems. We can translate the knowledge and skills back to such problems, especially those concerning the necessities of life and social difficulties. This then enables us to construct a curriculum taking such problems as a point of departure and a guide. When practical problems are used to furnish and structure the curriculum and when we involve the pupils in solving or surmounting such problems, we provide the intended reconstruction of experience. When we also supply them with the necessary materials, means and support, the result will be education as it should be.

Dewey warns that this kind of education is much more complex and laborious than traditional education and typical educational reform. Designing and programming this is extremely complex and labor-intensive because, besides the necessary knowledge of subject content and subject history, it requires knowledge of the development of children's capabilities and interests and of how this development can be systematically and continuously influenced by bringing children into contact with practical problems. For instance, we must know in which order, which specific practical problems are suited to 'cross-fertilize' the development of certain children with the development of certain knowledge or skills. Furthermore, besides all the knowledge regarding subject content and child development, considerable degrees of resourcefulness, creativity and skill is called for, in order to design real, concrete

---

[200] Ibid., 11.

education (activities, materials, organization, learning environment et cetera) surrounding the chosen specific practical problems. In short: it is not easy to produce such education. But it is worth the effort: it provides an "organic connection" between the world of the child and the realm of the subject matter; it prevents "lack of motivation", because the knowledge and skills are used immediately and hence constantly prove their use; and the subject matter does not have to be simplified or jazzed up.[201] The familiar contrasts evaporate.

In the book The Child and the Curriculum Dewey doesn't describe what educational should actually look like in practice. In a number of other texts he is more practically oriented, for instance in the texts on the Laboratory School[202] and in the book School and Society.[203]

All learning takes place through activities in response to problems, preferably in connection with fulfilling necessities of life or preventing or rectifying social problems. Dewey calls these activities "occupations":

> "By occupation I mean a mode of activity on the part of the child which reproduces, or runs parallel to, some form of work carried on in social life."[204]

When speaking of primary education, Dewey is thinking of activities such as carpentry, cooking, sewing and weaving. Occupations combine motor activities with observation, weighing alternatives, assessing, planning, reflection, decision making et cetera. Experience, thought and action interact. That is what learning is, according to Dewey: this dynamic of experience, thought and action. It builds upon the assumption that pupils are active and are given the necessary scope for this, especially:

> "(I)ntellectual responsibility for selecting the materials and instruments that are most fit, and ... opportunity to think out his own model and plan of work, led to perceive his own errors, and find out how to correct them."[205]

---

[201] Ibid., 24-26.
[202] Cf. J. Dewey, The University School. University (of Chicago) Record, 1, Nov. 1896, 417-419, also in: J.A. Boydston (Ed.), The early works of John Dewey, 1882-1898: Vol. 5 1895-1898: Early Essays (pp. 436-441). Carbondale/Edwardsville: Southern Illinois University Press, 1972; J. Dewey, The Chicago Experiment, in: K.C. Mayhew & A.C. Edwards, The Dewey School: The Laboratory School of the University of Chicago, 1896-1903. New York/London: D. Appleton Century Company, 1936.
[203] J. Dewey, School and Society. Chicago/London: University of Chicago Press, 1899
[204] Ibid., 131.
[205] Ibid., 132.

The nature of occupations guarantees their educative nature. Whether they are appropriate, motivating and educative depends on the selection and planning of the occupations: which activities pupils are to do, at which level, when, and in which sequence and in which context. The guidelines for selection and planning naturally have to do with, on the one hand, the pupils' capabilities, prior knowledge and experience and their needs, concerns and interests and, on the other hand, the origins and historical development of the knowledge and skills to be mastered. It goes without saying that in primary education, one should start close to home and with elementary things. This explains the emphasis, during the first school years, on for instance "house-keeping", "wood-work", "foods" and "clothing".[206] In his Plan of Organization of the University Primary School published in 1895, Dewey gave starting points for organizing 'occupations' for each theme. Take for instance "Wood-work":

> In the case of "Wood-work" Dewey first names thirty kinds of wooden things, such as breadboard, drying rack, chicken coop, chest, closet, stool, serving tray, boat and house. Next, of the top of his head (or so it seems), he lists a series of activities, often just as headwords, which contribute to the production of the things mentioned –production in the broadest sense of the word.
>
> It goes something like this: "Study teacher's model or invent one. Discuss materials. Study woods. Collect woods. ... Visit carpenters and wood-workers. Study growth of wood in the tree. Life of the tree. Observe trees of the locality. ... Markets of lumber. Prices. Transportation. Fossilized wood. Cost of labor connected with lumber. Study of lumber as building material compared with stone, brick, etc. ... Write and read records of observations made. Write and read stories and descriptions of subjects related to work. Draw and paint illustrations. ... Draw working plans. ... Make exact estimates of work to be done and statement of work that has been done. Cost –to one child– for class. Keep accounts and bills. Order and buy materials. Learn prices of woods –causes of difference. Learn cost of labor – reasons. Learn cost of transportation –reasons."
>
> After that, connected but more specific activities are listed by subject, for the subjects "Arithmetic", "Botany", "Chemistry", "History", "Physics", "Zoology", "Geography" and "Geology and Mineralogy".[207]

---

[206] J. Dewey, Plan of Organization of the University Primary School. In: J.A. Boydston (Ed.), The early works of John Dewey, 1882-1898: Vol. 5 1895-1898: Early Essays (pp. 224-243). Carbondale/Edwardsville: Southern Illinois University Press, 1972.
[207] Ibid., 233-237.

For Dewey, the educational value of occupations was beyond dispute. Forty years after the Plan of Organization, thirty years after ending the experiment in Chicago, he still believed in them, at least in the underlying principle:

> "Occupations as engaged in by the pupils themselves were means of securing the transformation of crude and sporadic impulses into activities having a sufficiently long time-span as to demand foresight, planning, retrospective reviews, the need for further information and insight into principles of connection. On the moral side, this same continuity demanded patience, perseverance, and thoroughness all the elements that make for genuine as distinct from artificially imposed discipline."[208]

Occupations teach foresight, planning, retrospection, judgment, searching for and gathering knowledge and insight, patience, perseverance and precision. Everything else children have to learn at school can be learned in the context of occupations; at least, in theory and in principle. Dewey's concrete practical proposals didn't go beyond elementary education. In hindsight, Dewey admits that even this was actually an impossible task:

> "The pressing problem with respect to 'subject matter' was ... to find those things in the direct present experience of the young which were the roots out of which would grow more elaborate, technical, and organized knowledge in later years. The solution of the problem is extremely difficult; we did not reach it; it has not yet been reached and in its fullness will never be reached."[209]

Nevertheless, the Laboratory School-experiment illustrates what Dewey meant by occupations. In his later work, Dewey sticks to the principle. For instance, it figures again in Experience and Education from 1938, when Dewey discusses the "organization of subject matter". It is recognizable in Dewey's characterization of the educational learning process:

> "Problems are the stimulus to thinking ... Growth depends upon the presence of difficulty to be overcome by the exercise of intelligence. ... It is part of the educator's responsibility to see equally to two things: First, that the problem grows out of the conditions of the experience being had in the present, and that it is within the range of the capacity of students; and secondly, that it is such that it arouses in the learner an active quest for information and for production of new ideas. The new facts and new ideas thus obtained become the ground for

---

[208] J. Dewey, The Chicago Experiment, in: K.C. Mayhew & A.C. Edwards, The Dewey School: The Laboratory School of the University of Chicago, 1896-1903. New York/London: D. Appleton Century Company, 1936, 474.

[209] Dewey, The Chicago Experiment, 468, 469.

further experiences in which new problems are presented. The process is a continuous spiral."[210]

Learning is the reconstruction of experience through solving problems by the exercise of intelligence. Solving problems yields new knowledge and ideas which, in turn, automatically generate new problems, which, yet again, can be solved by intelligence. The curriculum should amount to a program of problems, of problems that gradually require more knowledge and skill in order to be resolved.

Dewey holds his own particular view on the curriculum. It should be composed of occupations, activities in response to problems, preferably problems connected to providing the necessities of life or preventing or solving social problems. Dewey's point of view puts into perspective and transcends the contrasts between the supporters of the traditional curriculum who give priority to cultural transmission, and the education reformers who put the development of the child first. Dewey also distinguishes himself from reformers who view the promotion of social efficiency as the core function of education. The occupations are not pre figurations of vocations and Dewey is not arguing in favor of systematically training pupils in socially useful activities.

Contrary to Dewey, Parkhurst does not have a personal outlook on the curriculum, except that it there is no necessity to reform it. Dalton assignments translate the subject matter into portions of individual work. They don't change anything about the subject matter, just the way the subject matter is presented to the pupil. The curriculum remains the same. Dewey's occupations constitute the subject matter and hence also the curriculum. Educational reform, in accordance with Dewey's theories, is not possible without a thorough overhaul of the traditional curriculum. Parkhurst wished not to become involved in the discussion on subject matter and curriculum. It is questionable whether she did justice to her pedagogical ideas in this way. There are three reasons for this.

The first reason, we already mentioned in the previous paragraph. Parkhurst overlooks the fact that learning general and comprehensive skills through experience, according to her own requirements, would demand programming; therefore it couldn't really work without a curriculum.

In the second place, Parkhurst occasionally reveals that she nonetheless holds certain pronounced views concerning the curriculum. She is, for instance, in favor of "synthetic education", interdisciplinary or integrated education, a kind of education in which the subject boundaries fade due to presenting the knowledge and skills of

---

[210] Dewey, Experience and Education, 79.

the various subjects in such a way as to make visible mutual relations and reciprocal influences. This makes subject matter come alive and be fertile. A certain book recommending "synthetic education" is extensively quoted by Parkhurst; she calls it "a little book with a big message".[211]

The third reason is more complex. Parkhurst believes we shouldn't indoctrinate:

> "We must not limit the pupil by chaining him to our ideas, but we must set him free to make discoveries and permit him to have ideas of his own."[212]

Good education should make sure that pupils do not adopt our ideas, but form their own instead. "No more spoon-feeding," Parkhurst calls it. It is a classic educational principle that turns up in Parkhurst's texts here and there, for instance when she criticizes nationalistic and patriotic history education[213] and when recommending the availability of rich and diverse reference and source material in every subject room.

> "Nothing could be more valuable in the development of the pupil's intelligence than the opportunity ... of comparing the different views of different authors on the subject he is studying."[214]

Is Parkhurst not overly optimistic about the feasibility of promoting freedom of thought and judgment in education without putting specific demands upon the subject matter and curriculum? Surely, history education would require content changes in order to become less nationalistic or patriotic. And wouldn't the subject matter change as soon as pupils study and compare various different books, instead of using one particular method exclusively?

Dewey would have found Parkhurst too optimistic. For him, the freedom to think and judge is part of the "freedom of intelligence", the only kind of freedom of lasting significance.[215] This freedom only thrives in an education totally infused with experience, "educative experience", and so only in education guided by experience that meets the criteria of continuity and interaction. We have seen how determining this is for subject matter and curriculum. In Dewey's case, the development of "freedom of intelligence" is therefore dependent on the content of the occupations and on their imbedding and sequence.[216] The curriculum is therefore the decisive

---

[211] EDP, 30 ff.
[212] TES, July 30, 1921.
[213] EDP, 71.
[214] EDP, 40. TES, July 16, 1921.
[215] Dewey, Experience and Education, 61.
[216] Chapters 5, 6 and 7 in Dewey, Experience and Education.

factor in the advancement of the freedom of thought and judgment. Dewey saw this more clearly than Parkhurst.

For Dewey, content is the decisive factor, for Parkhurst it is form. The practical consequences are interesting. An example of this takes us back to the primary difference of opinion between Parkhurst and Dewey. According to Parkhurst the school contributes to democracy and sociality by providing social experience: "interaction of group life", mutual dependence and involvement; it is the organizational form that makes all the difference. When Dewey asks himself how education might contribute to democracy and sociality, he thinks of educational content, subject matter and curriculum. A case in point is his lecture Social purposes in education, held in 1922.[217] According to Dewey, education has three social objectives: citizenship, making a living and meaningful use of leisure time. These are more or less familiar aims, but should be interpreted more broadly than usual:

> Education for citizenship ought to be more than gaining knowledge about politics, "the machinery of government".[218] Pupils require insight into social and economic influences and power relations, the field of influences in which politics operate and are part of. Especially the dominant role of commerce and industry and the financial sector deserve attention, much more so than is customary in education.

> Equipping pupils for making a living should go further than vocational preparation.[219] In Dewey's opinion, being "capable of one's own support" should preferably be interpreted more broadly when viewed as an educational objective. Ideally, a young person develops "reserves to meet emergencies, to stand on his own feet, and to use his own hands, directed by his own brain". It is a broad and practical everyday notion concerning the ability to do things independently and it requires a different curriculum than customary in the average school.

> Education should not only prepare for citizenship and independence, but also for the meaningful use of leisure time. "Worthy use of leisure" has been an officially acknowledged educational aim since 1918 in the United States.[220] Dewey considers it to be a social aim. "Preparation for our leisure

---

[217] J. Dewey, Social purposes in education. In: J.A. Boydston (Ed.), The middle works of John Dewey, 1899-1924: Vol. 15 1923-1924: Journal articles, essays, and miscellany published (pp. 158-169). Carbondale/Edwardsville: Southern Illinois University Press, 1983.
[218] Ibid., 158-163.
[219] Ibid., 164-167.
[220] As a finding of The Report of the Commission on the Reorganization of Secondary Education. See Kliebard, 96, 97.

is an increasingly important part in training for good citizenship".[221] People have increasingly more free time on their hands. In Dewey's opinion this is not always spent usefully and worthily; too many people, especially the young, cannot think of anything better to do with it than "having a good time". A good citizen can employ his time "in a socially profitable way": "He is a person who has the capacity for appreciation of art, science, history, and literature for their own sake".[222] Once more, it is a question of subject matter and the curriculum.

All three aspects of the social aim demand a revision of educational content. As crucial as the form is to Parkhurst, the curriculum is to Dewey.

Recapitulating: the differences between Parkhurst and Dewey with respect to the school as a community, learning through experience, education through activities and the curriculum are of a fundamental nature. Parkhurst often employs a phraseology closely related to that of Dewey. But they are not on the same wavelength, neither in a practical nor a theoretical sense.

In her article in Times Educational Supplement, Parkhurst ridicules reformers who poorly understand Dewey and follow him fragmentarily:

> "Some teachers considered themselves followers of Dewey when they but made toy-villages and played at society on a miniature scale. They fell far short of the fundamental philosophy."[223]

According to Dewey, the school should be a miniature society. Dewey was referring to the necessity of founding education on occupations, corresponding to activities in real life and society. When they simply play mini society, mini democracy, mini shop, mini post office or the like, this is certainly a sign of ignorance.[224] We have to conclude, however, that Parkhurst herself fell short in her understanding of Dewey. There is a further conclusion warranted. In a few places in her texts, Parkhurst suggests that her insights and methods correspond to those of Dewey. In those instances, it is lip service, at the very most. The differences are too profound.

---

[221] Ibid., 167-169.

[222] Ibid., 167. Dewey perhaps sounds archaic and pedantic in the way in which he expresses his opinion of how the people and youth spend their free time. This is, however, a generally accepted opinion among academics during the first half of the twentieth century.

[223] TES, July 2, 1921.

[224] It also happens nowadays that one plays democracy at school with an appeal to Dewey (pupil participation, co-management) as practice in citizenship. This appeal is not justified; as such a practice is not in accordance with Dewey's opinions.

7 Montessori

The Dalton Plan is often considered to be a version of the Montessori Method: as if the theory and practice of the Italian education reformer were the guiding force in Parkhurst's educational reform. This is a misconception. As an educational practice, the Dalton Plan developed independently from Montessori. It was practically ready when Parkhurst first came into contact with her.[225] It is, however, plausible that Parkhurst was influenced by Montessori as to the theoretical justification of the Dalton Plan. In the years prior to writing Education on the Dalton Plan, Parkhurst was intensively involved with Montessori's work and that she had great respect for her expertise and talent.

Nowhere in her book, has Parkhurst referred to Maria Montessori (1870-1952). Their collaboration between 1915 and 1918 is only mentioned indirectly.[226] Such step-motherly treatment fails to do justice to the collaboration, nor does it do justice to the kinship of their ideas.[227] We shall compare the approaches of Montessori and Parkhurst with regard to three crucial points: individual work, individual choice and the role of the teacher. Then we shall examine how elementary ideas of Parkhurst's relate to Montessori's thought and practice. But first we shall briefly sketch the flirtation between Parkhurst and Montessori.

Liaison

In the years of 1912, 1913, the Dalton Plan nears its completion and is being tried out at the Edison School in Tacoma. In the same period, progressive America discovers the Montessori Method, a child-friendly approach which gives rise to exceptional learning achievements in children. It quickly becomes a hit. The enthusiasm of progressive opinion leaders spreads to the general public. One of the early day fans is the publisher and writer McClure, owner of the popular McClure's Magazine. He flatters Montessori by calling her an "educational wonder worker" and he regularly pays attention to her work in his magazine. McClure arranges for Montessori to come to America towards the end of 1913 for a lecture tour.[228] The tour is a success. When, in 1914, the enthusiasm reaches its climax, Parkhurst

---

[225] See chapter 1 Practical origins.
[226] EDP, 13, 14.
[227] It is more a sign of the discord with Montessori. See presently.
[228] G.L. Gutek, The Montessori Method. Lanham etc.: Rowman & Littlefield, 2004, 23 ff.

decides to travel to Italy to learn about the Montessori Method at first hand.[229] She wants to see it with her own eyes: "I just had to find out what Montessori knew about children that I didn't know."[230] Her partner, Luke, would later write: "She was not too happy about a foreign educator who threatened her rise toward supremacy in the field of child-education".[231]

In Rome, Parkhurst follows Montessori's international training course, a cycle of lectures and demonstrations. Parkhurst is immediately sold. She has to reluctantly acknowledge Montessori's superiority: "Maria Montessori was a mental giant whose energies were dedicated to the training of little children's minds, and as such she commanded my profound respect."[232] She experiences a strong like-mindedness. She recognizes her own ideas in Montessori's insights. And Montessori provokes her to form new ideas. Or, as Parkhurst puts it herself: through Montessori's words she becomes conscious of 'latent' ideas, "ideas that were yeasting in my unconscious".[233] Parkhurst experiences the course as extraordinarily inspirational and instructive. On her way home she concludes that the admiration for Montessori in America was not unfounded.[234]

When Montessori visits America a year later, the sympathy proves mutual. Montessori does her utmost to persuade Parkhurst to demonstrate the Montessori Method at the Panama-Pacific Exposition in San Francisco in 1915. Montessori doesn't speak English and needs a competent 'stand-in'. Parkhurst hesitates at first, owing to other obligations, but she ultimately agrees and subsequently dedicates herself to the task with enthusiasm. Montessori is very pleased with the way Parkhurst carries out the demonstrations. They agree to Parkhurst becoming her official American representative. For more than two years, Parkhurst devotes herself to spreading the Montessori Method, teacher education and training and improving the quality of Montessori schools. When, eventually, the combination of duties (Montessori ambassador, teacher educator, trainer, supervisor and inspector)

---

[229] In her autobiographical notes, Parkhurst suggests that she wished to go to Rome to meet the anthropologist Guiseppe Sergi. But this Sergi was one of the most important inspirational figures for Montessori. And once in Rome, she does not attend Sergi's lectures. There is a possibility that, looking back, Parkhurst attempted to downplay her interest in Montessori. Parkhurst and Montessori fall out with each other from the end of 1917 when Parkhurst no longer wishes to be involved in the spreading of the Montessori Method.
[230] Luke, 57.
[231] Luke, 57, 58.
[232] Ibid., 64.
[233] Ibid.
[234] Ibid., 70.

becomes too much for her, she withdraws, breaks with Montessori and resumes the thread of her own educational reform.[235]

Considering this liaison it shouldn't be surprising that the Dalton Plan is often seen as a variation of the Montessori Method.[236] Three other factors have contributed to this misconception. First: Parkhurst only began to develop the theory of Dalton plan after her Montessori period, giving the impression of her being dependent on Montessori. Second, the Dalton Plan is intended for pupils from nine years onwards, making it be readily conceived as a sequel to the Montessori Method which, at the time, was intended for the youngest pupils, up until about seven years of age. And third: there are similarities between the Dalton Plan and the Montessori Method, pertaining to both practice and theory.

In the following paragraphs, we shall look into this last point. There are, indeed, similarities but there are salient differences as well. We compare the Dalton Plan to the Montessori Method, as it was known to Parkhurst at the time she embarked on her collaboration with Montessori.[237]

---

[235] Parkhurst and Montessori fall out towards the end of 1917 when Parkhurst no longer wishes to be involved in the dissemination of the Montessori Method. Only after her death in 1952, Parkhurst starts to speak sympathetically about her once more. At an older age, she was even planning to write a biography on Montessori. Notwithstanding agreements with a publisher, the plan never materialized. (See for instance letters written to Van Willigen in the fifties and sixties. Present in the Dalton Archive of the Dutch Dalton Association (Nederlandse Daltonvereniging) and the Saxion in Deventer.)

[236] Misconceptions, for instance in: M. van Essen & J.D. Imelman, Historische Pedagogiek. Baarn: Intro, 1999, 117; L.C.T. Bigot, P.A. Diels and Ph. Kohnstamm, De toekomst van ons volksonderwijs. Part 2: Scholen met een losser klassenverband. Amsterdam: Nutsuitgeverij, 1924, 13; G. Geissler, Dalton-Plan, in: A. Paetz & U. Pilarczyk (Hg.), Schulen die anders waren. Berlin: Volk und Wissen Verlag, 1990, 12; H. Röhrs, Die progressive Erziehungsbewegung. Verlauf und Auswirkungen der Reformpädagogik in den USA. Hannover: Schroedel Verlag, 1977, 97; H. Besuden, Helen Parkhursts Dalton–Plan in den Vereinigten Staaten. Oldenburg: Sussman (Diss. Köln), 1955, 24. Cf. also: S. Popp, Der Dalton Plan in Theorie und Praxis. Innsbruck/Wien: Studienverlag, 1999 (Zweite Auflage), 63.

[237] Our source is once again the book De Methode Montessori of which the translation was published in America in 1912. See the following note. To be quite sure and to be complete, we checked the notes Parkhurst made in 1914 in Italy during the Montessori course to see whether these yielded a different image of Montessori's method and ideas. It is not always easy to decipher the manuscript, but the notes give the impression that the course did not contain anything new. A copy of the notes is present in the Dalton Archive of the Dutch Dalton Association (Dalton Archief van de Nederlandse Daltonvereniging) and the Saxion in Deventer.

Active learning

Learning is something children do themselves. According to Montessori, there are two crucial conditions: the availability of educative material and the freedom to work with it. When these conditions are met, learning proceeds automatically. A passage from The Montessori Method illustrates this approach:

> (The passage is about material for the development of the senses, meant for infants from two and a half to three and a half years-old.)
>
> "Let us suppose that we use... a block in which solid geometric forms are set. Into corresponding holes in the block are set ten little wooden cylinders, the bases diminishing gradually about ten millimeters. The game consists in taking the cylinders out of their places, putting them on the table, mixing them, and then putting each one back in its own place. The aim is to educate the eye to the differential perception of dimensions. ...
>
> (T)he normal child ... takes spontaneously a lively interest in this game. He pushes away all who would interfere, or offer to help him, and wishes to be alone before his problem. ... (T)he normal child attentively observes the relation between the size of the opening and that of the object which he is to place in the mould, and is greatly interested in the game, as is clearly shown by the expression of attention on the little face. If he mistakes, placing one of the objects in an opening that is small for it, he takes it away, and proceeds to make various trials, seeking the proper opening. If he makes a contrary error, letting the cylinder fall into an opening that is a little too large for it, and then collects all the successive cylinders in openings just a little too large, he will find himself at the last with the big cylinder in his hand while only the smallest opening is empty. The didactic material controls every error. The child proceeds to correct himself, doing this in various ways. Most often he feels the cylinders or shakes them, in order to recognize which are the largest. Sometimes, he sees at a glance where his error lies, pulls the cylinders from the places where they should not be, and puts those left out where they belong, then replaces all the others. The normal child always repeats the exercise with growing interest.
>
> Indeed, it is precisely in these errors that the educational importance of the didactic material lies, and when the child with evident security places each piece in its proper place, he has outgrown the exercise, and this piece of material becomes useless to him. This self-correction leads the child to concentrate his attention upon the differences of dimensions, and to

compare the various pieces. It is in just this comparison that the psycho-sensory exercise lies.

> There is, therefore, no question here of teaching the child the knowledge of the dimensions, through the medium of these pieces. Neither is it our aim that the child shall know how to use, without an error, the material presented to him thus performing the exercises well. That would place our material on the same basis as many others ... and would require again the active work of the teacher, who busies herself furnishing knowledge, and making haste to correct every error in order that the child may learn the use of the objects. Here instead it is the work of the child, the auto-correction, the auto-education which acts, for the teacher must not interfere in the slightest way."[238]

The quoted educational philosophy annex practice is characteristic for a substantial part of the Montessori Method as it was formulated prior to 1915.[239] Learning is something children do themselves, when given the opportunity to do so. That is: if there is educative material available and if they are given the freedom to use this material independently, or as Montessori calls it: if they are allowed the liberty to be active.[240] We shall now examine the two conditions: educative material and "liberty" as "activity".

The material must be educative. Working with it is obviously intended to broaden and improve knowledge and skills. According to Montessori, if the material is truly educative, then, by definition, it will also have other specific qualities. First: the material invites children of a certain age, in a certain developmental stage, to work with it. Second: the material holds the children's attention while they are using it; it stimulates activity and effort and this brings about concentration. Third: the material is self-corrective; by observing the material, the child notices when he has made a mistake, that it should be done differently, that he hasn't yet got it right et cetera. In short: educative material provides motivation, concentration and feedback.

Children have to be granted the freedom to work with the material. The Montessori teacher leaves the child to his own resources. More precisely: to the material and to the work. "The teacher must not interfere in the slightest way ... She must leave her

---

[238] M. Montessori, The Montessori Method Montessori. New York: Frederick a. Stokes Company, 1912 (Translation A.E. George), 169-173. (Italics in the original.)
[239] This is according to Montessori herself. We shall see later on that Montessori is not entirely consistent. Here we deliberately choose this book of Montessori's as an important source. It was published in 1912. This is how Parkhurst knew the Montessori Method at the time she developed her Dalton Education.
[240] Ibid, 86.

little scholars in liberty".[241] She doesn't have to teach the children anything, she doesn't have to hold their attention, to motivate and correct them, as all this is brought about by the material. Nevertheless, the teacher does have an important task. She provides the conditions. She ensures, for instance, that the appropriate material is available for use (neatly arranged, in order, visible, close at hand and suchlike), that the material is not used in an improper way (which would compromise its educative nature), that children are helped when they have trouble initiating their activities or if they get stuck during their work and that the children do not disturb one another too much. The teacher interferes as little as possible with the learning itself.

Based on her experiments, Montessori has high hopes for autonomous learning; she sees great advantages, for instance regarding discipline and the motivation to learn. Montessori believes that when the material is educative and children are given the freedom to work with it, they remain attentively engaged and repeat the exercise until they are saturated, as it were. The saturation point is reached when the child experiences that he is not learning anything new, hence when the material loses its educative character. The concentration occurring during the effort has a disciplining effect. The child works with dedication. He doesn't get distracted and has no inclination to distract others, to be awkward or to act up. The satisfaction, following the effort, motivates the child. He experiences that learning works, that his work yields results, that he learns something from it, that it increases his independence. This satisfying experience of mastery is conducive to the pleasure and interest with which the child embarks on more learning, in other words: with which he begins with new material, new work.

Parkhurst's approach resembles that of Montessori. The pupil will learn by himself as long as he has the opportunity to do so. What he needs are educative assignments and the freedom to work on these assignments. Then the pupil will learn. The teacher must let him do his work: "The more she teaches, the less will he learn".[242]
The teacher is modest and cautious when it comes to offering support; she is mainly concerned with the learning environment and materials. Parkhurst's justification sounds like Montessori's theory. She is equally optimistic: when pupils work on tasks independently, motivation, concentration and discipline come automatically. The similarity is merely superficial, however. Parkhurst's assignments differ profoundly from Montessori's materials. And Parkhurst's optimism regarding motivation, concentration and discipline has different underlying reasons than Montessori's optimism.

---

[241] Ibid., 172, 173.
[242] EDP, 65.

In Education on the Dalton Plan, Parkhurst explains what an assignment is and gives her own examples.[243] Parkhurst begins every assignment with an "interest pocket": a short introduction linked to the pupils' likely "needs and tastes", in order to encourage the pupil to embark on the assignment. Its function is to engage the pupil's attention and liven up the task.[244] The concrete examples of 'interest pockets' are, indeed, attempts to stimulate pupils to start working: by promising them that the work to be carried out will be interesting and relevant to them. Take the first example Parkhurst draws up:

> "MOTION AND FORCE
> Will an automobile start without an explosion of the gasoline? What makes a screw go into wood? Why do we oil our bicycles? Why do we use pulleys? Have you never wondered about these things? Daily we notice things that happen all about us, but seldom do we stop to consider how they happen! This month we are going to learn something about these common everyday happenings which are explained by certain fundamental laws in physics. We are going to consider some of the common types of machines and discover how they are able to accomplish the work that they do. In order to have a good understanding of machines it is important that we know something about motion and force. Therefore, in starting our work for the month we shall consider motion and force first."[245]

This appetizer is meant to tempt the pupils to spend a month occupying themselves, from time to time, with the laws of Newton by conducting a series of experiments, studying a chapter of the physics textbook and answering approximately thirty-five knowledge questions and questions requiring insight. Without a doubt, such instigation is necessary, for the work will not immediately appeal, attract and fascinate all pupils. After the interest pocket, the task commences with the suggestion to start by reading a paragraph in the physics book in order to learn about Newton's laws:

> "NEWTON'S THREE LAWS OF MOTION AND THEIR EFFECTS
>
> You will find it helpful to learn these three laws first and then proceed with the following experiments. (See reference 1.)"

---

[243] EDP, chapters 5 and 6.
[244] EDP, 59, 60.
[245] EDP, 75.

After this introduction, follows the first experiment:

> EXPERIMENT 1. A change of motion follows the direction of the force which causes it, and is proportional to the amount of force used and the time during which it acts.
>
> Directions: Suspend a small ball on a long string. Snap it at the same instant with one finger of each hand in directions that are at right angles to each other. Observe the direction in which the ball moves.

The function of the experiment is (apparently) modest. It serves as an illustration of the textbook knowledge. Directly after that, the pupil has to return to the book, before he begins with the other experiments.

> "Before undertaking the following experiments which have to do with the effects of Newton's Laws it is necessary to have some understanding of these effects. (See reference 2, and then verify your reading with the following experiments.)"

The following three experiments are again intended to illustrate the knowledge contained in the physics book, but now also to apply and process that knowledge. For instance the third:

> "EXPERIMENT 3. Momentum
>
> Directions: Using the same ball, roll it twice over the same surface, once slowly and once with speed. Note the distance that it travels. Now take two balls, one much heavier than the other, roll them over the surface, starting them at the same speed. Note the distances travelled."

After the fourth experiment questions are answered, for instance:

> "WRITTEN WORK
>
> Questions. (See references 1 and 2.)
>
> 1. State Newton's three laws of motion. Tell all that you know about Newton. (See reference 3.)
> 2. Give any examples of bodies that seem to set themselves in motion, and tell what outside force moves them. Why do we not find on earth any examples of constant motion without force being applied?

3. If two equal forces act upon a body in opposite directions, what would be the result? If the forces were unequal what would be the result?
4. What is meant by reaction? Could there be any reaction if there were no action? Is there ever any action without reaction?"[246]

Like the experiments, the purpose of the questions seems to be to help master and process textbook knowledge. The example given, constitutes the larger part of the first week's portion of work. The content and method of the other three week portions of the assignment are comparable: reading the textbook, conducting experiments, answering questions.

Such an assignment makes it possible to work independently and is certainly educative, but in other ways than Montessori's material. There are three salient differences.

First: contrary to Montessori's material, Parkhurst's assignments are not expected to inspire pupils to automatically start working on them when they are ready. The assignment requires an interest pocket. Pupils need to be convinced that working on the task is interesting and useful. The interest pocket serves to close the distance between the content of the work and the existing needs and spontaneous interest of the pupils. The need for interest pockets is one of the consequences of Parkhurst's decision not to become involved in discussions concerning the curriculum. Her reform has to fit any curriculum. The assignments do not replace or change the subject matter; they translate existing subject matter into portions of individual work, every possible subject matter. Parkhurst can therefore not assume or arrange that the content of the work is motivational in itself. The content has to be made attractive; hence the 'interest pocket' as "a vital feature of the assignment".[247]

The second difference has to do with the foregoing. The interest pocket provides the initial motivation. What ensures that the pupil, having started the assignment, remains motivated to do his best, to carry on working, to apply himself totally to the assignment, to resist distraction? In other words: what provides the motivation, the concentration and the discipline during individual work? In Montessori's case, it is the content of the activity: for instance manipulating cylinders. In Parkhurst's case, prolonged motivation, concentration and discipline is not dependent on the content of the activity. This doesn't differ so much from traditional education: reading books, illustrating knowledge and processing knowledge, answering questions. For her, it is, let's say, the 'exterior' of the work. Even when the content of the

---

[246] EDP, 75 ff.
[247] EDP, 59.

assignment fails to motivate, the assignment will motivate as a task in itself, the task as work.

> "It is not the job in itself but the challenging spirit of the job that commands the entire boy or girl. ... The very job has a halo. It awakens the inner child, a spiritual leaven begins to work; he feels the unfolding of his own powers, and he becomes self-disciplined by harnessing those same powers. He uses them to accomplish anything set before him. The best we can do is to encourage him and not interrupt the direction of his entire personality as it attacks first one thing and then another."[248]

Motivation, and also concentration and discipline, don't stem from the content of the work, but from the work as work. Parkhurst believes that the suggestion or experience of it being one's own work is of overriding importance here. The pupil takes the assignment upon himself; he enters into a contract.

> "Regardless of what that contract contains, the appealing, compelling thing, is the idea of a contract and the fact that he is in the role of voluntary agent to carry it out. He is custodian, not in custody, and he focuses his complete energies upon the task at hand."[249]

The assignment is "a real job", experienced as "my work", with emphasis on "my": that is what motivates[250] and facilitates concentration and discipline:

> "Conflicts cease, disorder disappears. The resistance ... is transformed into acquiescence, and then into interest and industry as soon as he is released to carry out the educational programme in his own way."[251]

The content of the assignment does not necessarily have to be interesting. Interest comes automatically in the course of the work. Parkhurst considers the fact that pupils become accustomed to this, an important advantage of the Dalton Plan:

> "(A) real preparation for life where we have to learn to do the work that lies before us whether we are interested in it or not. And even interest grows out of the sense of problems solved and obstacles conquered. As a child once remarked to a teacher whom I know: 'You learn that whatever you have to do can become what you want to do'."[252]

---

[248] TES, July 16, 1921. Cf. also EDP various places, for instance 23, 29, 43 and 155.
[249] TES, July 16, 1921. Cf. also EDP various places.
[250] TES, July 2, 1921. Cf. also EDP various places.
[251] EDP, 29.
[252] EDP, 145.

The third difference between the Parkhurst's assignments and Montessori's material is that pupils remain dependent upon the teacher while working on an assignment, for instance because the assignment itself is not self-corrective and doesn't give feedback. Assignments do not provide learning activities which keep themselves going and automatically come to an end when the pupil perceives that there is nothing left to learn. The assignment assigns activities which from time to time require the teacher's help and the assignment leads to results, for instance written answers, which are then assessed by the teacher. During an assignment, a pupil is sometimes requested to consult the teacher for further information, for instance: "After you have finished the required problems come to me and I will explain the next rule before you go on".[253] Frequently, the pupil is already tested and assessed while carrying out the assignment. For example: "Your problem this week will be to read about Nathan Hale, and then to come to me and let me test you on your reading". And a week later: "The problem is to read about John Paul Jones and then to come to me and give me an oral report on your reading."[254]

In her theory, Parkhurst alludes to assignment-work in which the pupil follows his own initiative and corrects himself:

> "What does a pupil do when given ... responsibility for the performance of such and such work? Instinctively he seeks the best way of achieving it. Then having decided, he proceeds to act upon that decision. Supposing his plan does not seem to fit his purpose, he discards it and tries another."[255]

In her practice it doesn't work like this. At least, the examples of assignments that Parkhurst elaborates are not such that the pupil would automatically notice if he didn't understand something or was on the wrong track. It is only in hindsight that, thanks to the teacher's feedback, the pupil experiences (perhaps per portion) how he carried out the work and whether or not he was on the right track. During the work, he would notice glaring mistakes at the most, and only in as far as these seriously interfere with the progression of the work.

Montessori contrasts her own learning materials with traditional materials that "require the active work of the teacher".[256] Parkhurst's assignments are such materials, learning materials requiring work on the part of the teacher.

---

[253] EDP, 60.
[254] EDP, 90.
[255] EDP, 23.
[256] Montessori, 172. See also previously.

Freedom of choice

Not only do Parkhurst and Montessori differ as to their conception of active learning and working independently, their ideas on choosing one's own work are also different. In both the Dalton Plan and the Montessori Method, the pupil himself chooses the assignment or the material on which or with which he is going to work. The reason differs. According to Montessori, a child is naturally attracted to material he is developmentally ready for. As long as the child is given the opportunity, the circumstances are good enough and the material supplied is suitable, the child will choose what is educative. The child chooses what his development requires.[257] This is the reason why the choice can be left up to the child. Indeed, for his reason the choice must be left up to the child. Once the Montessori teacher has adequately organized the environment and provided the correct supply of materials, nature will do the rest. The nature of the child is a more reliable measure of a child's needs and of what he is able to manage at a certain moment in time, than the teacher's assessment. It is sometimes necessary to help nature along, but this is something that only becomes apparent once the child has demonstrated that he is unable to carry on by himself.

In Parkhurst's work there are no traces of this specific faith in the natural development and natural disposition of the pupils. Parkhurst does appreciate the nature of the child, as most educational reformers do, but rather in the broad sense that children are naturally eager to learn and have good intentions, and they are able to do a lot without the assistance and interference of adults. Montessori bases her work on biological developmental theories and holds pronounced views on aptitude, maturation and sensitive periods; Parkhurst doesn't.

In the Dalton Plan it is for a different reason that pupils choose, from a certain number of alternatives, the assignment on which they are going to work. First, choosing for oneself promotes motivation and linked to this also concentration and discipline. Second, by choosing the activities himself, the pupil practices his skills in planning his own work and managing his time and he also gets used to responsibility. For instance, he learns to weigh up alternatives, to make judgments, decisions, judge consequences and adjust plans. Meanwhile, choosing one's own activities is obviously practical in differentiated education, which allows pupils to learn at their own pace and in their own way and gives pupils individual support. Such education is easier to organize when the pupil is partly responsible for what, when and how he learns.

---

[257] A.S. Lillard, Montessori. The Science behind the genius. New York: Oxford University Press, 2005, 107 and 122-126.

We have compared Parkhurst and Montessori on two points: working on one's own and making one's own choices. Characteristic of both the Dalton Plan and the Montessori Method is the emphasis placed on self-determined activity and pupils' independence; on activity that is directed and interrupted as little as possible by the teacher; activity using specially developed learning materials. The similarities, as we have seen, do not alter the fact that Parkhurst and Montessori differ strongly, both practically and theoretically. The next point of comparison concerns the role of the teacher.

Not much teaching

The teacher has an important role to play in the Montessori Method. This was already mentioned in the previous paragraph. The situation in which the pupil teaches himself, the 'auto education', places high demands on the educational setting and material. The Montessori teacher arranges this. For instance, she ensures that appropriate material is provided, in good order, in an organized fashion and within the pupils' reach. If necessary, the teacher also demonstrates how to work with the material. Furthermore, she helps pupils who experience difficulty starting up, or if they get stuck. She interferes as little as possible with the learning itself.

The Montessori teacher has a different role to that of the teacher in traditional education: "the teacher teaches little and observes much".[258] Observation is crucial in the context of timing and balancing her supervision. The teacher is modest and reserved, the pupils do the work. But intervening, interfering and directing as little as possible, without neglecting, without leaving pupils completely alone, means that the teacher has to have good knowledge of and also keep track of each pupil's needs. Besides knowing the pupils well and a thorough knowledge of the materials, this requires constant attention for what is happening in the class, for what the pupils are doing and how they are getting on with their work. Only then, the teacher is in a position to give timely and individually tailored advice and help: not too soon, not too late, not too generously, and not too sparingly.

Doing a lot of observation and not much teaching: that's hard for the average teacher. "To measure one's own activity ... is practically a very difficult matter. Especially is this true of teachers prepared by the old-time methods."[259] It is "a delicate task, a great art".[260] Not every teacher is up to the task. In The Montessori Method she gives several examples of, what she considers to be, blundering colleagues. Like the teacher who hastened to help a young boy, while he had just

---

[258] Montessori, i.a. 173.
[259] Ibid., 110.
[260] Ibid.,115.

found a solution to the problem of being too small to see what the other children were looking at:

> "I watched him from a distance with great interest; he first drew near to the other children and tried to force his way among them, but he was not strong enough to do this, and he then stood looking about him. The expression of thought on his little face was intensely interesting. I wish that I had had a camera so that I might have photographed him. His eye lighted upon a little chair, and evidently he made up his mind to place it behind the group of children and then to climb up on it. He began to move toward the chair, his face illuminated with hope, but at that moment the teacher seized him brutally (or, perhaps, she would have said, gently) in her arms, and lifting him up above the heads of the other children showed him the basin of water, saying, "Come, poor little one, you shall see too!" Undoubtedly the child, seeing the floating toys, did not experience the joy that he was about to feel through conquering the obstacle with his own force. The sight of those objects could be of no advantage to him, while his intelligent efforts would have developed his inner powers. The teacher hindered the child, in this case, from educating himself, without giving him any compensating good in return. The little fellow had been about to feel himself a conqueror, and he found himself held within two imprisoning arms, impotent. The expression of joy, anxiety, and hope, which had interested me so much faded from his face and left on it the stupid expression of the child who knows that others will act for him."[261]

Besides doing a lot of teaching and being too helpful, there is more the teacher is not allowed to do: she should refrain from rewarding and punishing and from giving orders and reprimands.[262] Well, not allowed ... There should be no need to do so. According to Montessori, there is no sense in rewarding. In a context in which they are taken seriously and are given the opportunity to work, children are not concerned about rewards. It even hurts their pride. Montessori illustrates this point with several examples as well. Such as the boy who didn't want a medal. A visitor brought a box of medals and said they were for the most well-behaved and best children.

> "At that moment, a most intelligent little boy of four, who was seated quietly at one of the little tables, wrinkled his forehead in an act of protest and cried out over and over again;–'Not to the boys, though, not to the boys!' What a revelation! This little fellow already knew that he stood among the best and strongest of his class, although no one had ever revealed this fact to him, and he

---

[261] Ibid., 92.
[262] Ibid., 101 ff. and 346 ff.

did not wish to be offended by this prize. Not knowing how to defend his dignity, he invoked the superior quality of his masculinity!"[263]

Punishment helps just as little as rewarding. According to Montessori, the only effective punishment for misbehavior, is setting the child apart. But this should be carried out in an affectionate way, with things on the table for him to do, and enabling him to still see the other children. This method of separation always helps, Montessori writes. The child calms down and seeing his fellows is "an object lesson much more efficacious than any words of the teacher could possibly have been".[264]

'Keeping order' is generally not necessary under the Montessori Method. Discipline comes naturally along with motivation and concentration:

> "(D)iscipline could never be obtained by commands, by sermonizing, in short, through any of the disciplinary devices universally known. ... To obtain ... discipline it is quite useless to count on reprimands or spoken exhortations. ... The first dawning of real discipline comes through work. At a given moment it happens that a child becomes keenly interested in a piece of work, showing it by the expression of his face, by his intense attention, by his perseverance in the same exercise. That child has set foot upon the road leading to discipline."[265]

When the pupils are given the opportunity to work, the teacher does not have to enforce discipline. The materials provide work, and consequently: discipline. The policy of not punishing and rewarding and not giving orders and reprimands fits the habit of refraining from correcting pupils during their work. While the pupil is working, he is automatically corrected by the material. When, in the course of the lesson, the pupil lacks certain knowledge, makes a mistake or does something wrong, then also the teacher does not correct.

> "(If the child) makes a mistake, she must not correct him, but must suspend her lesson, to take it up again another day. Indeed, why correct him? "[266]

According to Montessori, a correction is perceived by the pupil as a reproach. Reproach impedes learning, because it distracts. Suspending the lesson every time a pupil makes a mistake, would obviously be an unfeasible option during whole-class lessons. This kind of class teaching is not applied in the Montessori Method, or hardly so.[267] Teaching is only offered to a one pupil at a time or else to a small

---

[263] Ibid., 103.
[264] Ibid., 103.
[265] Ibid., 349, 350.
[266] Ibid., 226.
[267] According to Montessori's book, to which we are still referring: The Montessori Method.

number of pupils. Characteristic qualities of the lessons are "brevity, simplicity and objectivity".[268] Usually the lessons are meant to introduce working with the material. For instance as instruction: how to use the material. Or as an elaboration: the teacher's contribution as part of working with the material.

An example of the latter is a spelling exercise. The child has cardboard or leather letters in a box in front of him. The teacher then utters a word; "she pronounces very clearly a word; ... very distinctly, repeating the sounds a number of times".[269] The child lays the letters on the table: the correct letters in the correct order. At first the child needs help, but he soon gets the hang of it.

> "It is most interesting indeed to watch the child at this work. Intensely attentive, he sits watching the box, moving his lips almost imperceptibly, and taking one by one the necessary letters, rarely committing an error in spelling. The movement of the lips reveals the fact that he repeats to himself an infinite number of times the words whose sounds he is translating into signs"[270]

In this kind of lesson the teacher and the material together constitute the learning material, as it were.

Although Montessori consistently rejects whole class instruction, in her description of the Montessori Method she still regularly gives examples of whole class activities which are intended to be educative. In such instances, Montessori often speaks of "exercise" or "play" instead of lessons. For example the exercise devised to learn the meaning of the number 0. The children sit on their chairs, grouped around the teacher.

> "I stand among them, and turning to one of them ... I say, 'Come, dear, come to me zero times.' The child almost always comes to me, and then runs back to his place. 'But, my boy, you came one time, and I told you to come zero times.' Then he begins to wonder. 'But what must I do, then?' 'Nothing; zero is nothing.' 'But how shall I do nothing?' 'Don't do anything. You must sit still. You must not come at all, not any times. Zero times. No times at all.' I repeat these exercises until the children understand."[271]

Montessori abhors whole class instruction, but she obviously has nothing against (what is now termed) 'class discussion'. And in the context of such a game or exercise or class discussion the teacher seemingly can instruct and correct. This seems

---

[268] Ibid., 108 ff.
[269] Ibid., 282.
[270] Ibid., 283.
[271] Ibid., 329.

inconsistent. It remains unclear how Montessori perceived this. The difference between these playful, class teaching methods and traditional forms of frontal class teaching is not discussed in the book The Montessori Method.

To some degree, the teacher in the Dalton Plan has a similar role to that of the teacher in the Montessori Method. The point of departure is identical: the teacher mainly provides learning conditions, particularly the learning environment and learning materials. She leaves the learning itself in the hands of the pupils themselves.

In Parkhurst's case, the teacher also offers little instruction. There are, however, daily group assemblies. Parkhurst speaks of "conferences" or "oral lessons". During these gatherings pupils ask questions and discuss their progress and the results of their work; the teacher gives clarification and feedback, explains things and introduces assignments. This is not an old-fashioned lesson governed by the teacher, but a form of cooperation between pupils and teacher; the pupils may also answer each other's questions, help and question each other.[272] The regularity and the structural nature of these class conferences (which are held every day, the same time, with the same purpose) distinguish the Dalton Plan from the Montessori Method.

In the Montessori Method the main task of the teacher is to observe, rather than instruct. For the Dalton teacher observation is less important. Her pupils are somewhat older: being children and young people from nine years upwards, while Montessori starts with toddlers. In the Dalton Plan the teacher doesn't constantly have to infer what the children are experiencing and what they are developmentally ready for. She can rely on what the pupils say and ask for. In the Dalton Plan the teacher can therefore let her support depend upon explicit signs and the pupils' own initiative. More so than in the Montessori Method, the pupils can be left to their own devices while working. The teacher remains present and available, but doesn't need to keep track of everything or to develop a very thorough understanding of the pupils.

Nevertheless, the Dalton teacher should familiarize herself with the pupils, their backgrounds, their capabilities, their interests and the progress of their activities. For instance, because she has to advise pupils with their planning, when necessary, and to help them when they have trouble organizing their work, and because she designs the assignments and has to take into account what her pupils are capable of, what they are developmentally ready for and what interests them. The teacher must therefore have an eye for her pupils, listen to them, understand what inspires and motivates them. This doesn't mean she has to continuously observe the pupils. Parkhurst assumes that daily interaction and experience with the pupils will give the teachers

---

[272] Cf. e.g. EDP, 55.

sufficient information. This is one of the reasons behind the principle of 'co-operation' or 'interaction of group life'. The free social interaction between the pupils and the teacher has a positive influence on the contact between teacher and pupils. The Dalton Plan also provides a specific form of monitoring. The pupils fill in on charts which tasks they have completed. These graphs are read by the teacher in order to keep track of the pupils' progress.[273]

In education according to the Dalton Plan it is no more necessary to keep order than in education according to the Montessori Method. As was already described, Parkhurst expects that the assignment as work will lead to motivation, concentration and discipline. Furthermore, she assumes that the community character of school life will prevent the pupils from being a nuisance to others; at least they will not learn to be a nuisance to others. After all, 'interaction of group life' regulates behavior, according to Parkhurst.[274] Thanks to the learning materials and the way they work together, the teacher doesn't have to worry about the pupils' behavior. That is one less concern, which also applies to Montessori and for the same reasons.

As opposed to the Montessori Method, correction and feedback are the work of the teacher in the Dalton Plan. Parkhurst does not share Montessori's objections towards this. And her learning material doesn't take this work off her hands: Dalton assignments are not as consistently and completely equipped for 'autoeducation' as Montessori materials are. In the Dalton Plan, the pupils have their work checked, assessed and if necessary corrected by the teacher.

Regarding the role of the teacher, the most fundamental difference between Parkhurst and Montessori is that, in the Dalton Plan, it is the teacher herself who designs the assignments, whereas, in the Montessori Method, the teacher uses prescribed materials. Montessori impresses upon the teachers that they should follow her method as precisely as possible; the materials developed by Montessori are an integral part of the method. The Dalton Plan does not provide ready-made tasks. This would not match the openness and flexibility Parkhurst has in mind. Fixed tasks would tie the Dalton Plan to a certain curriculum, which is not what Parkhurst wants. She offers teachers guidelines and examples, enabling them to make their own assignments befitting the curriculum of their own school, the content of their own subject and the characteristics of their own pupils.[275] Ideally, the teachers should cooperate when devising the assignments. The tasks may then be harmonized and relations between the various subjects can be made visible. Moreover, when the

---

[273] Cf. TES, August 6, 192 and EDP, chapter 7.
[274] Cf. e.g. EDP, 18-23 and 43.
[275] EDP, chapter 5.

teachers make the assignments together, they can combine their knowledge of the children.[276]

Making assignments requires a certain expertise with respect to subject content. This is an important reason why Parkhurst prefers subject teachers.[277] In Montessori's case the teacher must have knowledge of the prescribed materials. Montessori would prefer the teacher to be a generalist, or even better: a Montessori-specialist, instead of a subject specialist.[278] Once a teacher has become sufficiently familiar with the Montessori Method, she will no longer require subject knowledge. This is because the Montessori Method not only comprises of a specific method and predetermined materials, but linked to this, also supplies a tailored curriculum: a specific Montessori curriculum with specific Montessori learning content. At the time Parkhurst was first introduced to the Montessori Method, the curriculum only catered for the first couple of years of school life. Initially, the Method was meant for toddlers and infants, children up to about 7 years of age. Later on, Montessori further develops her method, including corresponding learning materials and curriculum. The contrast with Parkhurst is evident. In her Dalton Plan, Parkhurst consciously chose to restrict herself to (what she calls) the organization of education; she doesn't wish to comment on content (curriculum and subject matter) or become involved in discussions on educational reform. She leaves the curriculum as it is.

Efficiency, aims, experience, freedom and sociality

We have now compared Parkhurst and the Dalton Plan to Montessori and her method, regarding three issues: active learning, freedom of choice and the role of the teacher. In order to complete the comparison, we wish offer a short account of how Montessori's theory and practice relate to Parkhurst's elementary notions: efficiency, learning to live and learning tit work, learning by experience, freedom and sociality.[279]

The Dalton Plan is meant to make the usual school learning more efficient. For Montessori efficiency is not a priority. Her main aim is to bring education into line with the nature of the child, or more precisely: with the way children naturally learn. Of course Montessori believes her method works more efficiently than all other methods, but this is not a priority for her. This line of thinking would also seem more at home in the American context than in the Italian context. In the following chapter we shall learn how much, during the first decades of the twentieth century, the Americans were under the spell of the ideology of efficiency. Parkhurst explicitly

---

[276] EDP, 61 ff.
[277] Cf. e.g. EDP, 49.
[278] Lillard, 146.
[279] Cf. Chapter 2 The theory of the Dalton Plan.

responds to this. It doesn't mean anything to Montessori and there is no need for her to consider it.

Education should allow the pupils to prepare themselves for life and work, according to Parkhurst. In this sense, she hardly departs at all from the standard view of that era. Montessori opts for a different perspective, but ultimately arrives at the same point. Education should help children to educate themselves; 'autoeducation', as she calls it. According to Montessori, the direction in which the child's learning is headed is determined the child's inner motives and not by what is considered useful and socially or culturally valuable. The future doesn't set the standard for education. The child's nature is the norm. This seems different than in Parkhurst's case. But, all things considered, there's not much difference. Children are naturally bent on gaining more and more independence, Montessori believes: they seem to be motivated by a strong will to be able to get by without the help of others. And for Montessori, learning is by definition a matter of work: working with materials. Learning, according to Montessori's approach, is therefore practicing and preparing for life and work. We can influence its direction through the organization of the learning environment and the choice of materials. Because, however much children may be incited by inner motives, they don't learn in a vacuum, but always through what they encounter in their environment. Regarding the organization of the learning environment and the choice of materials, Montessori is guided by what counts as socially and culturally useful, such as, following and besides the development of the senses and motor skills: hygiene, good manners, housekeeping, reading, writing and arithmetic[280] and later mathematics, grammar and music.[281] Lo and behold, Montessori's and Parkhurst's wishes boil down to the same in the end: education practices living and working and prepares for life and work. For both of them: education is in order to learn to live and to work.

To live and to work is best learned by experience. "Experience is the best and indeed the only real teacher", Parkhurst believes.[282] For Montessori this is just as obvious as it is for Parkhurst. Her method is entirely tailored to provide this: teaching oneself ('auto education'); all by experience. Montessori is more consistent than Parkhurst in this respect, as pupils are less dependent upon the teacher, particularly due to the fact that Montessori's material is self-corrective and provides feedback.

Freedom is a prerequisite for experience. For Parkhurst freedom is a crucial working principle of good education. In this context, freedom means: the opportunity to do

---

[280] Cf. M. Montessori, The Montessori Method.
[281] Cf. M. Montessori, The Montessori Elementary Material. (The Advanced Montessori Method. Part II). London: William Heinemann, 1918.
[282] EDP, 152.

the work, to do the work oneself, to organize it oneself (how, where, when) and to work at one's own pace, and to not be disturbed while working. For Montessori, this is no different: "Liberty is activity".[283] Learning is something children do themselves when they are given the opportunity: there has to be educative material at hand and freedom to work with it. For both Parkhurst and Montessori, freedom is a requirement for concentration, motivation and discipline. Besides all similarities in this area, there is one difference. In Montessori's case, there is an additional aspect. For Montessori freedom also means spontaneity. It is the cornerstone of her method, she writes: "studying the pupil before educating him, and of leaving him free in his spontaneous manifestations".[284] Freedom, taken in this sense, is essential for education placing great emphasis on the natural development of the child. After all, the less scope there is for spontaneity, the less natural the development. In this context, Montessori stresses the relationship between freedom and observation. With an eye to natural development, the teacher promotes, respects and monitors the pupils' freedom. She does this mainly by observing instead of mostly instructing: she follows the activities of the children meticulously and only intervenes when she is certain the child is hindering his own learning process.

Like Parkhurst, Montessori takes the trouble of pointing out that freedom has its restrictions. Parkhurst writes that the pupil may not just do as he pleases: "The child who 'does as he likes' is not a free child"; freedom has to do with "the pursuit and organization of his own studies in his own way".[285] Self-activation legitimizes and regulates freedom. For Montessori, freedom is equally relative.[286] Her freedom, with its connotation of spontaneity, has definite limits too. We should not suppress the spontaneous actions of the child, for "perhaps we suffocate life itself," Montessori writes[287], but...

> "The liberty of the child should have as its limit the collective interest; as its form, what we universally consider good breeding. We must, therefore, check in the child whatever offends or annoys others, or whatever tends toward rough or ill-bred acts".[288]

In both Parkhurst and Montessori's case, pupils' freedom is pedagogical (functionally) and educational (morally and conventionally) limited.

---

[283] M. Montessori, The Montessori Method, 86.
[284] Ibid., 15.
[285] EDP, 18, 19.
[286] Montessori, 86 ff.
[287] Ibid., 87.
[288] Ibid., 86, 87.

In her early work Montessori pays little attention to the social aspect of education. Parkhurst considers this a serious omission. In her Education on the Dalton Plan she states it as the reason for the rift between Montessori and herself:

> "I felt I had devoted sufficient study to the individual aspect of education. The school in its aspect of a human society then engrossed my energy."[289]

Parkhurst clearly endorses a common contemporary criticism of Montessori: the Montessori Method is viewed as being too individualistic, not sufficiently social. Three critical notes are called for.

First: the Dalton Plan later on is subject to similar criticism. The Dalton Plan is deemed to be too individualistic as well.[290] The criticism concerns the emphasis placed on individual learning. Pupils work individually on Parkhurst's assignments, equally individually as with Montessori's materials. The learning materials of both Parkhurst and Montessori are not designed to facilitate cooperative learning among pupils.

Second: in her book The Montessori Method, Montessori actually does draw attention to social education. Various exercises combine learning to read, write or calculate with learning to cooperate. In a game for learning to read, for instance:

> The children take a rolled up piece of paper out of a box with the name of a toy on it. They read it out loud and are then allowed to take the toy. But after that, they have to take turns to choose another piece of paper from a box. This time it has the name of a younger fellow pupil on it, who is not yet able to read and therefore doesn't have a toy. The name is read aloud and the toy taken earlier is handed to this fellow pupil.

> "We taught the children to present these toys in a gracious and polite way, accompanying the act with a bow. In this way we did away with every idea of class distinction, and inspired the sentiment of kindness toward those who did not possess the same blessings as ourselves."[291]

---

[289] EDP, 14.

[290] Cf. H. Röhrs, Die progressive Erziehungsbewegung. Verlauf und Auswirkungen der Reformpädagogik in den USA. Hannover: Schroedel Verlag, 1977; H. Besuden, Helen Parkhursts Dalton–Plan in den Vereinigten Staaten. Oldenburg: Sussman (Diss. Köln), 1955; S. Popp, Der Dalton Plan in Theorie und Praxis. Innsbruck/Wien: Studienverlag, 1999 (Zweite Auflage).

[291] Montessori, 299.

Giving away what you have just received. That is not very natural behavior. Neither is containing oneself in the face of disappointment. This, too, is something children have to learn in Montessori education, in this case as a lesson on the side during an exercise in remembering numbers.[292] It's not natural, but certainly social.

Third: Parkhurst believes that socialization and learning to cooperate will occur automatically when the natural interaction among children is not hindered. As soon as school customs and rules no longer stand in the way of 'interaction of group life', the pupil will automatically function "as a member of a social community"; by doing and by experience he learns to associate with others, to consider others and to realize he is responsible for the whole. Although in her theory Montessori pays no explicit attention to this socializing function of education, the Montessori practice looks like the Dalton practice in this regard. For instance, the children choose their own materials and, in doing so, have to consider each other. Pupils move freely around the classroom; they look at each other's work and talk among themselves. In this way, Montessori counts on them learning from and through each other: they copy each other and learn how the materials are meant to be used by observing others, and they let themselves be motivated by what others are doing and achieving and they let themselves be motivated by the criticism and admiration of other children. The organization of the learning environment and the nature of the learning materials are different in the Montessori Method than in the Dalton Plan, but the pupils' freedom of movement and opportunity to interact freely or naturally with fellow pupils are equal for both practices. Parkhurst would have to agree that the two methods are equally socializing.

The comparison undertaken in the present and the preceding paragraphs, demonstrates that there are indeed resemblances between Parkhurst and Montessori, but also significant differences. Three examples of similarity are: a) the freedom on the part of the pupils; b) the emphasis on independent and individual learning by using specific learning materials; c) the faith in the motivating, disciplining and educative effects of active learning. Three examples of differences are:

a) In the Dalton Plan the teacher's role is significantly greater than that of the teacher in the Montessori Method. Parkhurst's assignments are not 'auto educative', at least not to the extent that Montessori's materials are.

b) Parkhurst believes that activity has an intrinsic motivational and disciplinary effect, irrespective of the content of the activity (hence: of what the pupil is doing). According to Montessori this does depend on the content of the activity, particularly on the relationship between the activity

---

[292] Ibid., 331, 332.

and natural development. It depends on what the child is ready for in terms of his natural development.

c) In the Dalton Plan the teachers create the assignments themselves, and together with colleagues; they are tailored to the characteristics and circumstances of their pupils. In doing so they adhere to the curriculum of the school. In the Montessori Method ready-made materials are used. These are attuned to the natural course of development of the child (the average child) and correspond to the characteristic Montessori curriculum. The teachers follow the method closely.

Taking the differences into consideration, it is not obvious that the Dalton Plan could pass for a variant of the Montessori Method.

8 Taylor and Bobbitt

The Dalton Plan is an "efficiency measure". It aims at being a "simple and economic reorganization of the school", which creates optimal conditions for education, that is to say: for "the teacher to teach and the learner to learn".[293] With the emphasis on efficiency, Parkhurst conforms to the spirit of her era. Her image of efficient education is, however, diametrically opposed to then-current conceptions of efficient education. She seems to oppose Taylor's and Bobbitt's scientific management.

Scientific management

Efficiency was in vogue in America. The period 1910-1920 is retrospectively named the "Age of Efficiency".[294] The pursuit of efficiency had its roots in industry. Production processes were improved by systematically and accurately researching what would be the quickest and most economical manufacturing procedures, and to adjust and control these accordingly. A crucial factor in this context was the optimalization of labor processes. To this end, the daily work routines of workers were analyzed. These were dissected into as many distinct actions as possible. For each specific action it was subsequently analyzed how these best to be executed, that is to say: the fastest and the most economical along with maximum yield. In this way detailed action prescriptions were devised. By combining the prescriptions for the various specific actions, it was mapped in great detail how the composite actions could be optimally executed. This was the standard based on which the worker was instructed, directed, assessed and rewarded.

Scientific management is based on this approach. It became well-known through the work of Frederick W. Taylor (1856-1915). According to Taylor, for every job there is just one best procedure and the only way to determine this, is by conducting scientific research. The workers own hands-on expertise and practical rules of thumb cannot match the scientific study of their work routines. In scientific management a standard work routine is devised, based upon job analysis and this standard is subsequently used in the selection and schooling of employees. Employees are trained to carry out their work in full compliance to the standard prescriptions. They are not permitted to act according to their own judgment and considerations; they are not allowed to go by their own routine and skill. They are obliged to follow the

---

[293] EDP, 34 and 45; TES, July 2, 1921; TES, July 9, 1921.
[294] R.E. Callahan, Education and the cult of efficiency. Chicago/London: The University of Chicago Press, 1962, 42.

given instructions without fail. Each employee is allocated a task by the planning department. The task prescribes exactly what has to be done, how it has to be done, when it has to be done and how much time it has to take. In his book The principles of scientific management, published in 1911, Taylor summarizes this as follows:

> "Perhaps the most prominent single element in modern scientific management is the task idea. The work of every workman is fully planned out by the management at least one day in advance, and each man receives in most cases complete written instructions, describing in detail the task which he is to accomplish, as well as the means to be used in doing the work. ... This task specifies not only what is to be done but how it is to be done and the exact time allowed for doing it."[295]

The management is responsible for virtually everything: the planning, the processes, the control and the work methods, et cetera. The employee just has to do what he is instructed to do, exactly what he is instructed to do.[296]

Scientific management emerged around the turn of the century among engineers. The results in terms of cost reduction and output were promising. It rapidly gained ground in the fields of industry, commerce and construction. Scientific management quickly became popular in all sectors of society, including education. The most important exponent in the field of education is Franklin Bobbitt (1876-1956).

According to Bobbitt, the school is highly suited for improvement in terms of efficiency and scientific management. Education is a production process: "a shaping process as much as the manufacture of steel rails".[297] Teachers are the workers; the pupils are the raw material. The school should be run like a business: based on scientific research and organized from the top down. The school management determines what has to be done, how it is to be done and when and to which end; the teacher executes.

> "The directive and supervisory members must clearly define the ends toward which the organization strives. They must co-ordinate the labors of all so as to attain those ends. They must find the best methods of work, and they must enforce the use of these methods on the part of the workers ... Directors and

---

[295] F.W. Taylor, The principles of scientific management. New York: Harper and Brothers, 1911, 39.
[296] Callahan, 25-34.
[297] F. Bobbitt, Twelfth Yearbook of the National Society for the Study of Education. Part I. The Supervision of City Schools. Some General Principles of Management Applied to the Problems of City-School Systems. Bloomington, Ill.: Public School Publishing, 1913, 11. Quoted in: Callahan, 81.

supervisors must keep the workers supplied with detailed instructions as to the work to be done, the standards to be reached, the methods to be employed, and the materials and appliances to be used."[298]

Bobbitt is optimistic about the possibility of objectively and precisely determining, externally and top-down, how teaching should be carried out. As in determining prescriptions and standards for industry and construction, it is a matter of precise and systematic observation and analysis. In efficient education, teachers are not led by their practical experience and expertise; they don't act according to their own judgment and considerations, but closely follow the methods prescribed by managers. Just like other employees under scientific management, they conform to specified standards, are compared and judged on the basis of these standards, and are selected and schooled with an eye to these standards.[299]

Bobbitt is equally optimistic regarding the possibility of objectively and precisely determining what should be taught. In Bobbitt's opinion, the controversy concerning the content of the curriculum (see previously: chapter 6 Dewey, paragraph Subject matter and the curriculum), may be resolved in a simple and impartial manner:

> "Human life, however varied, consists in the performance of specific activities. Education that prepares for life is one that prepares definitely and adequately for these specific activities. However numerous and diverse they may be for any social class, they can be discovered. This requires only that one go out in the world of affairs and discover the particulars of which these affairs consist. These will show the abilities, attitudes, habits, appreciations, and forms of knowledge that men need. These will be the objectives of the curriculum. They will be numerous, definite, and particularized. The curriculum will then be that series of experiences which children and youth must have by way of attaining those objectives."[300]

What has to be taught can be determined by a form of job analysis. The life that education prepares for can be broken down into a series of specific activities. What children and young people have to learn, in the course of time, are the skills, attitudes and knowledge presupposed by these activities. A proportion of these are usually learned automatically, in and outside the home. The remainder requires school learning. This is what the school should address, no more than this.

---

[298] Bobbitt, 7, 8. Quoted in: Callahan, 80.
[299] Bobbitt, 23-96; Callahan, 79-91. For a discussion with more solid critical understanding see: F. Bobbitt, Discovering and Formulating the Objectives of Teacher Training Institutions. Journal of Educational Research, 10, 1924, 187-196.
[300] F. Bobbitt, The Curriculum. Boston: Houghton Mifflin Company, 1918, 42.

Incidentally, in practice Bobbitt opted for a different approach.[301] To work out what the curriculum should look like, he made use of a number of surveys. In the course of a few years, he asked about fifteen hundred of his own students at the University of Chicago to report which skills, attitudes and knowledge they thought necessary in modern adult life. Based on the results he drew up an extensive list of subjects and objectives. He then let twelve hundred secondary school teachers critically examine this list. What remained was a series of approximately five hundred items, varying from making a campfire and selling your car at a profit to 'doing your best irrespective the circumstances' and the willingness to obey laws, besides basic skills such as arithmetic, reading and writing. Bobbitt's position in the curriculum debate is strongly utilitarian: societal usefulness is given great weight. It counts as the most significant version of the 'social efficiency'-approach.[302]

Efficiency and responsibility

Due to Taylor and Bobbitt, in America between 1915 and 1925, educational reform with a view to efficiency is associated with, first, scientific management and second with utilitarian curriculum-development based on job analysis-like research. This is completely different to what Parkhurst has in mind. She is opposed to scientific management, or it would seem so at least. Nowhere does Parkhurst mention it by name, but she unmistakably challenges it. She doesn't become involved in discussions about the content of the curriculum. Like Bobbitt, she believes that education should prepare for adult life, for work and social living; she does not think, however, that this requires changes to be made to the curriculum.[303]

Parkhurst is opposed to the scientific management approach to education. She holds a radically different opinion concerning the role and the responsibility of the teacher. In the Dalton Plan the teacher is his own boss, his own manager. He doesn't indiscriminately follow instructions imposed by superiors and outsiders. He formulates his own education. For instance, he puts together his own assignments.

---

[301] F. Bobbitt, How to make a curriculum. Boston: Houghton Mifflin Company, 1924. See also: B.H. Bode, Modern Educational Theories. New York: The Macmillan Company, 1927, 73-93.

[302] See for the positions in the curriculum debate: chapter 6 Dewey, paragraph Subject matter and the curriculum. Cf. also Kliebard, 83, 84 and 98-102 and Bode, 73-121. Bobbitt's position in the debate is, of course, controversial, for instance on account of the underlying method (seeking consensus by means of questionnaires), the variability of 'objectives' (for instance very specific opposed to rather vague) and the curious assumption that culture and society are unchanging (as if, at this moment of time, we would know what the next generation needs in terms of knowledge, attitudes and skills).

[303] See chapter 2 The theory of the Dalton Plan, paragraph Learning to live and learning to work.

This is, however, not the essence of the difference between the Dalton Plan and scientific management. The actual contrast is on another level.

For Parkhurst the school is a community of workers, just as it is for Bobbitt. A fundamental difference with Bobbitt is that the in the Dalton Plan the teachers are not the only workers. It is especially the pupils who do the work. They learn. There is nothing made out of them; they are not raw material. They work themselves. Parkhurst speaks of their schoolwork in terms of jobs and contracts. In the Dalton Plan the work is placed in their own hands; or rather: the pupils take on the work. Schoolwork in the form of assignments is work accepted, work taken on.

There is another difference. According to the theory of scientific management, the efficiency of a labor organization increases when its employees are given less responsibility for what they are doing, how they are doing it and when they are doing it. Parkhurst turns this round. We increase efficiency in education through a reorganization in which the responsibility of the pupil as a person taking on work is extended instead of restricted. We should let the pupils take the work into their own hands and at the same time give them the responsibility to determine for themselves how they wish to do their work and how they plan it, and so: when they do what. The strong emphasis in the Dalton Plan on the pupil as someone who takes on work and personal responsibility, who adheres to his chosen work method and time management, is diametrically opposed to Taylor's idea of efficiency.

Parkhurst does not refer to Taylor, but considering her reversal of the image of efficient education, she could clearly have responded to a line of reasoning of Taylor's, set forth in his book Shop Management published in 1912:

> "There is no question that the average individual accomplishes the most when he either gives himself, or someone else assigns him, a definite task, namely, a given amount of work which he must do within a given time; and the more elementary the mind and character of the individual the more necessary does it become that each task shall extend over a short period of time only. No school teacher would think of telling children in a general way to study a certain book or subject. It is practically universal to assign each day a definite lesson beginning on one specified page and line and ending on another; and the best progress is made when the conditions are such that a definite study hour or period can be assigned in which the lesson must be learned. Most of us remain, through a great part of our lives, in this respect, grown-up children, and do our best only under pressure of a task of comparatively short duration."[304]

---

[304] F.W. Taylor, Shop Management. New York: Harper and Brothers, 1912, 69.

Taylor believes workers are unable to handle responsibility and therefore need specified tasks with a precise planning in short units of time, because they are like big children: they cannot handle broad assignments and are unable to organize their own time. Parkhurst's line of reasoning is the exact opposite to this. Pupils can indeed bear responsibility, they don't have to have everything repeated over and over again and they are able to plan their own work; as long as teachers are prepared to take the little workers seriously.

The Dalton Plan, with its emphasis on responsibility for one's own work, seems to be intended to make pupils proof against scientific management. Or to make them unsuited to employment under scientific management.

In Education on the Dalton Plan Parkhurst tells a story confirming our suspicions concerning her criticism of scientific management. In order to understand our interpretation, we need to explain something about the historical context, a detail really. In 1910, Taylor became known to the general public due to a mounting conflict concerning the railroads. According to one of the parties the management of the railroads was not efficient. If scientific management was implemented, significant savings could be achieved, without lowering the wages of the railroad workers.[305] In the railroad debate, Taylor was named as an economic wonder doctor and his method of increasing the efficiency gained fame as an economic panacea. It can hardly be a coincidence that, in the beginning of her book, Parkhurst writes about an enlightening train journey.

She tells of how she became involved in a conversation with a fellow passenger, who held an office job with the railroads. He pointed out to her a group of railroad workers:

> "Look at those men ... they've not the slightest idea of the best way to handle their work. ... Because the handling of the job belongs to the foreman. It is his duty to think for the gang. A labourer who thinks for himself would soon be voted a nuisance. ... Yet how much better the result would be if the labourer looked upon the job as his own and felt responsible for it. In that case the foreman would become a helper instead of a driver."[306]

The fellow passenger obviously had little appreciation for scientific management. Workers, who don't slavishly carry out orders, but show responsibility for their work, achieve better results. When Parkhurst asked what he thought about his boss, the director of the railroad company, he was lyrical:

---

[305] Callahan, 19 ff.
[306] EDP, 8.

"Oh! He's another sort altogether. We've a president who knows how. He looks ahead and plans with that rare ability built up by experience. Why, when he begins to talk you soon find he's left you and your ideas as far behind as this train has left those labourers. Yes, our president's one in a million, a fearless human being!"[307]

The boss knows how it should be done, he knows how to plan and he is resourceful. And this is all based on experience. The boss represents the exact opposite to the worker under scientific management. This made a profound impression on Parkhurst:

"The phrase sank into my heart, for isn't that just what we educationalists are trying to create, fearless human beings? Life needs them, the world needs them because there are never enough to go round. They are so rare those men and women who can look ahead and plan, who know how!"[308]

The message is clear. The railroad workers should be made responsible for their work. Actually, they should all resemble the railroad director. There shouldn't be just one person like the boss: everyone should be like the boss. That is what the world needs, what life needs. And that's what education is for.

"Fearless human beings", people who are up to anything. That is what education should aim to achieve. Parkhurst reiterates the characterization when, following Emerson, she idealizes the city boys as "the masters of the playground and the street".[309] They are dexterous, worldly-wise, and smart and think ahead; and it's all due to experience. The director of the railroads[310] and the boys in the street; these are examples. Enterprising people are what we need. This is very different to the efficient component parts of Taylor and Bobbitt's scientific management theory. Parkhurst advocates efficient education. But for her, efficient education is more or less the opposite of what, thanks to Taylor and Bobbitt, is usually meant by this in her era.

---

[307] Ibid., 8, 9.
[308] Ibid., 9.
[309] EDP, 26, 27.
[310] In order to prevent misunderstanding: the director of the railroads at that time in America was different to a railway director nowadays. Around 1900 the railroad industry was at the peak of industrial progress.

9 The theory revisited

In the previous chapters we have depicted the historical-theoretical context of the Dalton Plan by comparing the practice and theory of Parkhurst with ideas on education and reform to which she refers: those of the poet cum philosopher Emerson, the developmental biologist Conklin, the psychologist Swift, the educational philosopher Dewey, the education reformer Montessori and the efficiency researchers Taylor and Bobbitt. In this chapter we shall discuss the outcome. First we shall consider how Parkhurst relates to then contemporary science, research, theory development and discussion on education. We then summarize our findings.

Experiment and science

In the comparison with Emerson and Conklin, we noticed that Parkhurst did not always understand what she read or else wasn't always a very careful reader. Or perhaps she didn't always read everything. This impression is confirmed by a passage found in Luke's biographical notes. In bursts Parkhurst read many books, so many that Luke wondered where she found the time. The answer is telling:

> "I rarely finish a book. When I come across something that gives me a creative idea, I usually close the book and that's the end of it for me."[311]

She was pragmatically oriented in her reading. Parkhurst's main interest was the practice of education.[312] Her educational reform was not the application of theoretical understanding or philosophical insight. The Dalton Plan originated in practice and was based on practice. The theory was developed retrospectively. The innovation itself was an experience based educational reform.

Parkhurst's approach to educational reform can be distinguished from two other forms of experience based improvement of education: that of Emerson and those of Dewey and Montessori.[313]

Emerson did not think highly of reforms. Education is not improved by changing the school or the materials or the didactics or the curriculum. Education, according

---

[311] Luke, 161.

[312] See chapter 1 Practical origins, paragraph Practical and down-to-earth.

[313] Cf. respectively chapters 3, 5, 6 and 7.

to Emerson, will only improve as the teacher gets better. More precisely: when the teacher improves himself. The more tact, patience, respect and wisdom he demonstrates in teaching, and in his approach towards pupils, the better his education will become.[314] This is promoted by professional experience. If the teacher is sensible enough, he will gradually improve himself through his teaching. An appeal may help: an appeal to the teacher's professional ethos may stimulate reflection.

Contrary to Emerson, Parkhurst believes that improvement starts with reform, especially reforming the ways in which education is organized. In this context organization refers to learning environment, learning materials, class management and pedagogics. Parkhurst thinks that once education is organized differently, teacher behavior and attitude will adapt automatically.

Parkhurst experimented with organizational reform: reform of learning environment, learning materials, class management and pedagogics. She was not the only one to experiment with education. Dewey and Montessori did too, along with many others at that time. Education was improved by trying things out in practice. The content of the experiments differed from one reformer to the next, but the nature of the experiments could also differ considerably. Some experiments were scientific: testing hypotheses, developing theories. Other experiments were practical, primarily aimed at alleviating urgent problems. Parkhurst's experimenting is an example of the latter. It is embedded in practice. It is not so much concerned with science and theory. Parkhurst may well have been inspired and encouraged by theories and science in some respects, but her experiments have no systematic relationship with scientific research or theory formation, in spite of her contacts with academics.[315]

Dewey and Montessori are different in this respect. Both view their educational experiments as scientific experiments. For Dewey the Laboratory School is a true laboratory: created to test theories on teaching and learning.[316] Something similar applies to Montessori. According to her, the Montessori Method is the result of pedagogical experiments and as far as she is concerned the further implementation of the method remains a form of experimental science.[317] Montessori views the study of the children's development in the Casa dei Bambini as a basic task of the Montessori teacher. This has everything to do with the emphasis placed on both the children's freedom and the teacher's observation: freedom is a prerequisite for authentic (natural and spontaneous) behavior and observation is the core activity in the study

---

[314] Cf. chapter 3 Emerson.

[315] See chapter 5 Swift, paragraph Science and practice. Cf. also chapter 1 Practical origins, the last two paragraphs.

[316] Cf. Dewey, The Chicago Experiment.

[317] Montessori, The Montessori Method.

of that behavior.³¹⁸ Dewey and Montessori both have scientific aspirations. It is unclear to which extent they succeeded in working scientifically. But that's a question we need not answer here.

As far as aspirations are concerned, Dewey and Montessori represent the ideal of the psychologist Swift: improvement of education linked to scientific experimental research.³¹⁹ Swift criticizes reforms that remain close to practice and that are mostly based on professional experience and professional initiative. He is therefore critical of reforms like Parkhurst's. She doesn't seem aware of this.³²⁰

For Bobbitt, too, it speaks for itself that educational reform should go hand in hand with scientific research.³²¹ He does, however, conceive the relationship between science and educational reform in a different way than Dewey, Montessori and Swift. Bobbitt believes that scientific research can determine how education should be and that these insights can subsequently be applied by adapting practice accordingly. Science offers guidelines and solutions; educational practice then accommodates to these. Bobbitt is optimistic as to the possibility of using scientific research to objectively and precisely determine the best educational learning methods and suitable educational content.³²² In this light, it is indeed befitting to conceive a technological or instrumental relationship between science and practice.

The biologist Conklin holds science in equally high esteem³²³, but is less optimistic than Bobbitt as to the possibility of objectively and specifically ascertaining what would best benefit education. Unlike Bobbitt, Conklin has an eye for the consequences of the fact that each child and every situation is different. Nothing is good or bad for everyone, as no one individual is the same as the next, Conklin warns. The best education is unique education, totally attuned to individual characteristics and situational factors. This can only be realized when everything is known of everyone individually, concerning characteristics and influences, circumstances and effects. It would require omniscient intelligence. This is not feasible, not even for science.³²⁴ Science cannot offer recipes, nor ready-made directives and solutions.

---

[318] See chapter 7 Montessori. Cf. Gutek, 43-45.
[319] See chapter 5 Swift, paragraph Science and practice.
[320] Ibid.
[321] See chapter 8 Taylor and Bobbitt.
[322] Ibid.
[323] See chapter 4 Conklin.
[324] Ibid. We place Conklin opposite to Bobbitt, because Conklin is cited by Parkhurst here, although not in connection with the relationship between science and practice. Bobbitt and Conklin have probably crossed swords, although regarding a different theme. Bobbitt

Like Conklin, Dewey, Montessori and Swift are modest about what science can do, more so than Bobbitt. Owing to this, their opinions also differ on what would be the ideal relation between science and practice. Whereas Bobbitt advocates and instrumental relationship, Dewey, Montessori and Swift believe science and practice would both benefit from a more dynamic and interactive relationship, a relationship allowing sufficient opportunity for interplay, so that science and practice would mutually inform each other, criticize, correct and stimulate each other.

Belief in science, as well as contributions to science, is distant from Parkhurst's practical orientation. Parkhurst is more interested in trying things out in practice and experiencing. For Parkhurst, experimenting in education is conducting practical experiments. She makes little use of science. This doesn't alter the fact that Parkhurst likes to make use of scientists, especially as 'sparring partners' in personal discussions (conversations and correspondence)[325] and as connections (networking) when it comes to promoting her work.[326]

Not involved in discussion

It fits her pragmatic attitude, that she is not passionate about theoretical reflection and discussion.[327] This is probably one of the reasons why Parkhurst doesn't participate in a number of then contemporary discussions on education which would certainly have been interesting to her and have had bearing on her work. We already mentioned several times, that Parkhurst remains aloof from the discussion on the curriculum.[328] It is at least as striking that Parkhurst doesn't comment on the Montessori criticism voiced by Dewey and Kilpatrick.

In 1914, the year that Parkhurst travels to Italy and reluctantly falls under the spell of the Montessori Method, Kilpatrick's book, The Montessori Method examined, is

---

was an advocate of eugenics, whereas Conklin was a prominent adversary. Cf. Callahan, footnote on p. 79 and chapter 4 Conklin. This contrast have everything to do with their difference of opinion concerning the relationship between science and practice: according to Bobbitt scientific research delivers unambiguous, immediately useful knowledge, whereas, according to Conklin, science demonstrates just how complex everything is and therefore how difficult it is to formulate unequivocal and general recipes.

[325] For instance the contacts with Burk and Bode. See chapter 1 Practical origins, the last paragraphs.

[326] For instance the contacts with O'Shea and later Kilpatrick. Ibid. Cf. also the correspondence between Parkhurst and O'Shea in the Dalton Archive of the Dutch Dalton Association (Nederlandse Daltonvereniging) and the Saxion in Deventer.

[327] See the beginning of chapter 2 The Theory of the Dalton Plan.

[328] For instance in chapter 6 Dewey, paragraph Subject matter and the curriculum.

published.[329] It is a shrewd study, based on an analysis of the book The Montessori Method and also on observations in Montessori schools, including in Italy. It clarifies, in an accessible way, what, according to Kilpatrick, is wrong with the Montessori Method.

The educational philosopher Kilpatrick, for instance, is extremely critical of Montessori's concept of development. Montessori has a limited understanding of development. She conceives it as the unfolding of "the child's nature as given at birth". As if "all that the child is to become" is already present at birth.[330] Such an image fails to do justice to the role of culture, "the funded capital of civilization", in development, Kilpatrick writes. She treats development as if it can occur independently of existent knowledge and skills, values, examples and models and suchlike.[331]

> "We must, therefore, reject Madam Montessori's interpretation of the doctrine of development as inadequate and misleading. The useful elements of this doctrine are covered up in error whenever development is identified with the mere unfolding of latency."[332]

At the same time, he believes that the nature of the child is not done sufficient justice by the Montessori Method. In her theory, Montessori is always talking of respecting the nature of the child, but her method actually fails to live up to this. There is relatively little scope for free expression, imagination, stories, drama and playing games, according to Kilpatrick.[333]

Precisely at that time in America, the enthusiasm for Montessori is at its climax.[334] The sharp critique doesn't go unnoticed. According to educational historians, Kilpatrick's verdict had an unfavorable effect on the introduction of the Montessori Method in America. It at least injured Montessori's good reputation:

> "Kilpatrick's stinging critique had a significant negative impact on the entry of the Montessori method into the teacher preparation programs in colleges and universities."[335]

---

[329] W.H. Kilpatrick, The Montessori Method examined. Boston: Houghton Mifflin Company, 1914.
[330] Ibid., 9.
[331] Ibid., 8.
[332] Ibid., 11.
[333] Ibid., 27-30.
[334] See chapter 7 Montessori, paragraph Liaison.
[335] Gutek, 33.

In the year Kilpatrick's book appears on the scene, Parkhurst returns from Italy as a Montessori apostle. In the following years, she makes a strong effort to spread the Montessori Method in America. How could it be, then, that she doesn't take the trouble of publishing a pamphlet or an article weighing and contradicting or putting into perspective Kilpatrick's arguments? Probably such an exercise was just too theoretical for her.

Parkhurst continues to ignore Kilpatrick's critique, also following her rift with Montessori, in arguing her own educational reform in Times Educational Supplement and Education on the Dalton Plan. Responding to Kilpatrick's objections and arguments would have been an obvious option, as they were well-known and also because of their relevance regarding Parkhurst's aims and arguments.

Kilpatrick, for instance, discusses the discrepancy between the ideal of 'auto education' and the use of Montessori material. According to him, the learning materials of the Montessori Method are so didactically solid and imperative, so unnatural, and the prescribed use is so forced and artificial, that free and spontaneous learning is practically out of the question and there can be only mechanical and artificial learning processes. It is "mechanical manipulation of very formal apparatus".[336] The same objection is put forward by Dewey a couple of years later in Democracy and Education.[337] Dewey and Kilpatrick both believe that 'auto education' demands activities that are less coercive and artificial, more natural and ordinary, than working with Montessori material in the correct way. Why does Parkhurst ignore Kilpatrick's well-known objections towards Montessori's learning materials in explaining and justifying the nature and function of her assignments? Parkhurst, too, aspires to a kind of education in which pupils educate themselves. She, too, turns to independent and active learning: allowing pupils to work for themselves with didactically well-conceived and prepared learning materials. Parkhurst must surely have wondered whether her Dalton Plan assignments were prone to the same objections as Montessori material. She must have at least realized that others will have asked themselves this question.

And why doesn't she make use of Kilpatrick's very favorable opinion of Montessori's conception of the freedom of the pupil and the way she makes it the keystone of her method? Kilpatrick establishes that Montessori pupils are given a lot of freedom, through which they grow accustomed to "self-reliance". He also observes that freedom benefits discipline and is conducive to the interaction and cooperation

---

[336] Kilpatrick, 33.
[337] Dewey, Democracy and Education, 160 and 205 ff.

among pupils.[338] Furthermore, he notes that freedom does not go at the expense of gaining knowledge and learning skills.[339] Kilpatrick has researched this thoroughly and can only conclude that Montessori is on the right track as far as freedom is concerned:

> "It is difficult, then, to escape the conclusion, from whatever standpoint we view the situation, that the relatively free expression of the child's natural impulses ... is the efficient plan for his proper rearing. Such freedom is necessary if the child is to enter with full zest into actual cooperation, and into the acquisition of those habits of knowledge and skill which are properly to be expected. The same freedom is necessary if he is to grow into adequate self-reliance, and, at the same time, into the adequate control of self in the appreciation of the rights of others. From such considerations we highly approve Madam Montessori's reemphasis of the doctrine of liberty. In the practical outworking of her idea she has set an example to home, to kindergarten, and to primary school."[340]

Virtually everything brought forward here by Kilpatrick concerning pupils' freedom, might have easily been exploited by Parkhurst in the theoretical vindication of freedom in the Dalton Plan.

One possible explanation for her ignoring Kilpatrick and the discussion on Montessori, we have already suggested: theoretical reflection and underpinning were not Parkhurst's forte and certainly not her passion. There is another feasible explanation. It is conceivable that Parkhurst had a specific audience in mind: that she was writing exclusively for practically interested readers and didn't want to bore them with theoretical discourse, hence she wished to spare them the theoretical stuff. But this, too, would imply that Parkhurst, comparatively speaking, attaches little importance to theoretical reflection and underpinning.[341] The historical theoretical contextualization of her work, such as we have undertaken here, would not have appealed to Parkhurst.

---

[338] Kilpatrick, 16 and 19-25.
[339] Ibid., 18, 19.
[340] Ibid., 25, 26.
[341] An alternative explanation might be that Parkhurst started to write at the request of interested persons from England and that she initially wrote for a British audience. Kilpatrick's book is less well-known than in America. This could explain why Kilpatrick was ignored in TES and EDP, but not for the comparative lack of theory in her work in general.

Efficient education

The objective of Parkhurst's educational reform is to achieve more efficient education. Considering her emphasis on efficiency, Parkhurst would seem to be at home within the tradition of Taylor and Bobbitt, that of scientific management. Actually, it turns out that she is opposed to this tradition. According to Parkhurst, education does indeed become more efficient through organizational reform. Efficiency does not increase, however, when teachers pass on their responsibility to managers; it increases when they make pupils responsible, responsible for their own work and jointly responsible for community living in the school setting.

Efficiency assumes clarity regarding purposes and goals. What is the goal of education? Like her contemporaries, Parkhurst believes that education should primarily be useful. It should allow children to practice, to get used to and to prepare for life, work and society. This means that education should contribute to the development and acquisition of knowledge, skills, virtues and habits deemed worthwhile and useful.

In addition to the broad objective, there is, in Parkhurst's case, also a more specific goal. In various places Parkhurst writes that education should aim towards bringing forth "fearless human beings", like the big boss of the railroads and the mischievous city boys. They are dexterous, skilled, quick-witted, experienced, worldly-wise, proactive and they think ahead. They are enterprising people.[342] This specific goal distinguishes the Dalton Plan from other educational approaches. In Dewey's case the ultimate objective is citizenship: pupils are to become active and constructive participants in society and culture. In Montessori's case, everything revolves around natural development: maturation and the unfolding of what is innately given. In Bobbitt's case it is all about socialization in the most commonplace sense of the word: the school reshapes unsuitable juveniles into socially and culturally suitable adults. In Conklin and Emerson's case, it is all about people making the best out of themselves; hence, the objective of education is 'exhausting talent' as it were; no promise or potential should remain undiscovered or undeveloped. For Parkhurst, education is about entrepreneurship and self-employment.

Besides Dewey's citizenship, Montessori's development, Bobbitt's socialization and Emerson and Conklin's flourishing, Parkhurst has her own view on what education should achieve. Education should ensure that children and youth become enterprising people and self-employed workers. This goal corresponds to the characteristic features of Dalton education. The Dalton Plan approaches pupils as enterprising and self-employed.

---

[342] See the last paragraph of chapter 8.

The curriculum is not the problem

Like others, Parkhurst doesn't believe that nineteenth century education is equal to the tasks it ought to be fulfilling. But, whereas her contemporaries, for instance Dewey and Bobbitt, mainly seek the solution in subject matter and curriculum reform, Parkhurst believes that the problem does not lie with the traditional subjects and subject content. In her opinion the problem is the organization of education. At least, there is a lot to be gained by improving the organization of education.

The defenders of the old school claim that being equipped for life, work and society is a natural outcome of typical scholarly knowledge and skills combined with typical school socialization and discipline. Traditional subjects and typical relations within the school would provide all the practice and ingredients needed.

Educational reformers in the Bobbitt tradition claim that the conservatives are mainly wrong when it comes to content. Traditional subjects are not tailored to the requirements of modern life, work and society. A different curriculum is needed. Progressive educational reformers maintain that the conservatives are completely wrong. Children and young people learn a lot at school. But education as it is, stands in the way of preparation for life, work and society; this applies to both content and form.

Parkhurst steadfastly follows her own mind. She believes that progressive educational reformers overestimate the problems, whereas reformers in the Bobbitt tradition underestimate them. In her opinion, the traditional curriculum cannot do much damage. It is indeed inadequate , but it does not necessarily stand in the way of preparation for life, work and society: provided that education is designed differently, to allow for a different kind of learning and socialization to occur. What's wrong with traditional education is its organization. This is where to look for the remedy. Any shortcomings pertaining to the curriculum may be compensated through the reorganization of education; the curriculum does not necessarily have to be changed. What does the organizational reform entail? It would at least guarantee experience, freedom and sociality.

Experience

Nothing is more educative than experience. Parkhurst shares this outlook with Dewey and Montessori and the majority of educational reformers. An obvious way of providing such experience is by making arrangements for active learning: enabling pupils to learn by allowing them to work for themselves. Dewey's occupations, Montessori's materials and Parkhurst's assignments have this function in common: the pupil is put to work. They choose different ways to achieve this.

In Montessori's case, the pupil works independently with the material. Each material comes with specific prescriptions which have to be followed. The intended experience is defined in detail in advance. If the pupil strays from the prescribed procedure, the material loses its educative nature. At the most the pupil will then learn something different than foreseen, as the experience will differ from the intended experience. The material is adapted to the pupils' natural development: it responds to it, follows it and contributes to it.

The Montessori Method provides a closed program of educative experiences; attuned to natural development. Dewey's ideal is an open program of educative experiences, geared towards the social and cultural development. It is not open in the sense of being free and spontaneous and learner-directed and lacking in for instance a curriculum. It is open in a different sense. In Dewey's occupations it is not predetermined when a pupil will experience something and what it will be exactly, but it is a certainty that he will have educative experience and what that experience will relate to, and so what he learns about. In Dewey's case, it is the curriculum, as a system and sequence of occupations, which guarantees that experiencing through occupations remains educative, hence that there is what Dewey calls an "experiential continuum", and that this is culturally and contextually on an appropriate level and up to date. It is the role of the teacher to supervise this process.

Parkhurst's assignments are of a different kind than Dewey's occupations. And working on assignments is of a different order than working with Montessori's material. The assignments transform subject matter into portions of individual work. Assignments do not make up the curriculum in the way that Montessori's materials together form her curriculum and in the way Dewey's occupations are to form a new curriculum. In Parkhurst's case it is the other way round: the existing subject matter is transformed into parcels of work to be carried out independently; the existing curriculum defines which subject matter is to be presented. Any subject matter and any curriculum would be suitable.

In working on assignments, learning by experience has to do with general and comprehensive skills, not with the subject matter itself. In other words: learning by experience does not have to do with subject content, but with subject transcending skills. For instance, through experience pupils learn planning skills, learn how to learn more efficiently or learn to show consideration for one another. Multiplication, geography or history, for instance, are still learned from books in an old fashioned way, by instruction, through practice, in processing and suchlike. Montessori and Dewey both aim at letting the subject matter itself, all the subject matter, consistently be learned through experience. For Parkhurst it suffices that a number of formal skills be learned in this way, through experience.

We might state this in a different way. In Parkhurst's case (a) the formal, comprehensive or general skills constitute a separate domain besides the traditional subject matter or existing subject matter, irrespective of which, and (b) skills are learned through experience, whereas subject matter is learned in other ways. Parkhurst believes that this would be feasible and worthwhile; that it is feasible and worthwhile to (a) learn general and comprehensive skills along with, but distinct from subject matter and (b) for these skills to be learned by experience, structurally and systematically, whereas the rest of the subject matter is learned in other ways. Montessori and Dewey clearly think differently about this. In their opinion the term general and comprehensive skills is nonsense: it is not possible to separate skills from subject matter. And in their eyes everything should be learned through experience.

In Parkhurst's case they form a separate domain, but a separate curriculum is not a prerequisite for the development of comprehensive skills. Parkhurst seems to place her trust in the idea that learning by experience in this domain occurs spontaneously or follows its own natural program or discovers its own effective pathway. The objective of experience based enhancement of comprehensive skills speaks for itself: being enterprising, which is Parkhurst's overriding educational goal. Or rather: remaining enterprising and becoming more enterprising. This is because, according to Parkhurst, it is a matter of development: children are naturally enterprising. Education just has to aptly respond to this, to promote it, and certainly not thwart it.

In the Dalton Plan the motivational and disciplining effects of active learning also occur at this general level. It is not the subject matter that motivates and disciplines. It is the work as work (job, assignment) that motivates and disciplines: planning the work, taking responsibility for it and suchlike. Or actually, it is the experience of doing this which has motivational and disciplining effects, the accompanying educative experience.

Freedom

In the Dalton Plan "liberation of the pupil" means that pupils are given the opportunity to do the schoolwork themselves, in their own way and at their own pace, and to plan the work themselves. Parkhurst believes that the pupil's freedom benefits his concentration, his motivation and his discipline. Swift and Montessori employ a similar concept of freedom and for the same reasons. Parkhurst, Swift and Montessori are very alike in this respect. There is a difference between Parkhurst and Montessori as to the practical execution. In the Dalton Plan the freedom of the pupil is limited by his cooperation with the teacher: the teacher offers support, gives feedback and assessment. In the Montessori Method the pupil's freedom is limited by the prescriptions for working with the material and by the strictly directive nature of the material.

Among other things, the importance of freedom has to do with individual differences among pupils and with the nature of the pupils. On this point, too, Parkhurst, Swift and Montessori are in agreement. Freedom facilitates variation, for instance variation in approach, level of work and work pace. In this way, freedom responds to individual differences, including natural differences. In this sense, Parkhurst, Swift and Montessori's concept of freedom answers to the concerns of Emerson and Conklin. Education that allows pupils too little freedom, easily fails to appreciate individual differences. This carries a significant risk of talent remaining unutilized and underdeveloped and not being given a chance to develop, which means that a lot of potential and promise would remain latent. Bringing the best out of every pupil requires "liberation".

As to the exact relations between freedom, concentration, motivation, discipline, variation and nature, there is a lack of clarity and also disagreement among the authors to whom Parkhurst refers. Although there is also some degree of similarity between Conklin, Swift and Montessori especially, Parkhurst herself is unclear and undecided in this area: she doesn't theorize and she doesn't take a particular standpoint. But for Parkhurst, it is beyond doubt that there is a connection, as it is for the others.

Freedom promotes concentration, motivation and discipline. And freedom facilitates variation. In this way, freedom does justice to the differences among pupils, for instance the natural differences. Meanwhile, granting freedom to the pupils is an indication of confidence, confidence in spontaneous, unconscious and natural processes. In nineteenth century education, pupils were granted little or no freedom: education for was a passive, mechanical and repressive affair.[343] The underlying thought was usually that everything pupils learn, at least all useful and valuable things they learn, is the result of purposeful activities on the part of the teacher, such as planning, explanation, instruction and correction. Everything depends on the teacher's efforts and on the inclination and ability of the pupil to simply follow the teacher. Towards the end of the nineteenth century the idea began to take root in wide circles that this is not the case. Useful and valuable learning is not totally dependent upon the teacher. Children and young people, partly automatically, learn much that is good and useful from one another too and also without teacher intervention, also outside the program, outside the lesson, outside the school et cetera. And these 'free' ways of learning might well work better than 'scholastic' learning methods, because they are more natural, personal, more down to earth,

---

[343] See the beginning of chapter 1 Practical origins, first paragraph: Her own schooldays.

more continuous and active. Dewey was one of the thinkers, the most well-known of these in fact, who systematically investigated the consequences of this for education.

Dewey's work demonstrates that putting one's trust in 'free' forms of learning doesn't entail that everything has to be left up to the pupils, nature and the force of coincidence. At the same time, based on Dewey's cautions and warnings to other progressive educational reformers, it is not hard to see how easy and tempting it is to succumb to this. All too frequently, and too much so, well-meaning reformers confused 'free' forms of learning with education lacking sufficient direction and structure. Parkhurst doesn't need to take Dewey's criticism personally: in the Dalton Plan the teacher and the curriculum, for the most part, retain their traditional directive and structuring functions.

Having too much faith in 'free' forms of learning is not a good thing; neither is too little. Having too little faith in 'free' forms of learning is characteristic of nineteenth century education, but it applies to Bobbitt's educational reform as well. He believes education to be a production process: the teacher makes something out of the pupils. What pupils learn is the result of effort on the part of the teacher. Bobbitt upholds the traditional notion that justifies a kind of education in which the pupil passively undergoes teaching, instead of actively learning. This is education in which the pupil's freedom is considered to be detrimental instead of a prerequisite. Bobbitt's approach is the opposite of Parkhurst's "liberation of the pupil".

Sociality

A general skill which pupils learn naturally, according to Parkhurst, is interaction in group life: interacting with one another, considering others, being conscious of one's responsibility for the common good. To achieve this, pupils generally do not require a teacher who instructs and corrects them, or a curriculum that programs them step by step. The only thing pupils need is the opportunity to gain experience. Hence, Parkhurst's "socialization of the school": which allows and enables pupils to interact and work together and with their teachers. On this point, Parkhurst's outlook corresponds to those of Swift and Montessori. It is a simple form of learning by experience. It also corresponds to Dewey's ideas, although Dewey is not content with pupils just learning to interact, being considerate towards others and conscious of their own responsibility for the common good. Dewey places higher demands on sociality: pupils must learn to live together democratically. This requires experience with cooperation. For Dewey, cooperation is the ideal, or even the true educational learning method. Judged by Dewey's standard, the Dalton Plan, like the Montessori

Method[344], is too one-sidedly aimed at working independently and individual development, and affords too little attention to cooperation.

Pragmatic, not guided by fundamental principles

Parkhurst was pragmatic to the core. She developed her Dalton education as a practicing teacher. The Dalton Plan was more or less ready in 1911; that is to say: practically ready. It took as long as about ten years for the theory to follow. The original Dalton education is not the application of a philosophy. We should therefore not interpret the theoretical justification of the Dalton Plan in terms of principles; at least, in terms of principles in the sense of convictions or underlying assumptions. We must understand the theory pragmatically; even the principles should be interpreted pragmatically. And that is perfectly feasible.

The word 'principle' has two meanings: first: 'fundamental principle' or 'maxim', such as in "principles of Calvinism", and second: 'working principle', as in "the principle of the two-stroke engine".[345] When Parkhurst uses the word 'principle' in her theoretical elaboration and justification, she denotes the second meaning. In reconstructing her theory, this is the most obvious interpretation. 'Freedom' and 'interaction of group life' are not principled (maxim-like), but functional (working principle-like): they are organizational reforms to make education more efficient.

In Europe this was not always grasped, and this definitely applies to Germany and the Netherlands. In the Netherlands Parkhurst's principles are always conceived as fundamental principles. This is still the case today.[346] In German-speaking regions the interpretation of Parkhurst's work suffers from the same shortcoming. The texts of the Austrian Eichelberger and the German Besuden are telling in this respect. In 2002 Eichelberger discusses the "Dalton-Prinzipien" as "Grundprinzipien".[347] As far as the first principle is concerned, "Freiheit", Parkhurst was, according to Eichelberger "wahrscheinlich beeinflusst" (probably influenced) by the four "Atlantische Freiheiten": "freedom of speech, freedom of religious worship, freedom from want and freedom from fear".[348] Hence, in Eichelbergers case, Parkhurst's

---

[344] Cf. Kilpatrick's critical commentary: Kilpatrick, 20.

[345] See the Van Dale Dutch dictionary. In English the variation in meaning is comparable. According the New Penguin English Dictionary i.a. 'principle' means "a universal and fundamental law, doctrine, or truth", "the essence or the basic idea behind something" and "a law or fact of nature underlying the working of a natural phenomenon or an artificial system or device".

[346] See for instance the website of the Dutch Dalton Association: http://www.dalton.nl.

[347] H. Eichelberger, Der Daltonplan. In H. Eichelberger (Hrsg.), Eine Einführung in die Daltonplan-Pädagogik. Innsbruck: StudienVerlag, 2002, 19.

[348] Ibid.

working principle 'freedom' is turned into a fundamental-human rights-like basic principle.

Besuden, too, calls Parkhurst's principles "Grundprinzipien".[349] In his opinion there are three: freedom, individuality and sociality ("Freiheit", "Individualität" and "Sozialität").[350] The second principle "Individualität" is not mentioned by Parkhurst herself, but Besuden deduces it from her practice and ideas. Three "Grundprizipien" are obviously too many for German thinkers: so there must be some deeper underlying principle. Besuden quotes Natorp with agreement: "Wo nicht ein Prinzip, da ist im strengen Sinne auch nicht ein PRINZIP erreicht".[351] What then, is the deeper, underlying principle of the Dalton Plan? As "leitende Idee" to which all the other basic principles can be traced back, Besuden chooses: self-development, "die Selbstentfaltung".[352] His line of argument is rather speculative: he doesn't show how his conclusion relates to Parkhurst's own statements. Self-development, as an ideal or objective or standard, does not figure in Parkhurst's reasoning. Aside from this, it is strange to interpret Parkhurst on even more principled level than principled; just to do it in a 'principled' way is already questionable enough.

In our opinion the German educational theorist Popp, remains more faithful to Parkhurst. She too formulates a "Grundprinzip", but her fundamental principle is more didactical, and is a better match to the Dalton Plan regarding content than Besuden's self-development and Eichelberger's political philosophy. Popp:

> "Das Grundprinzip besteht ... darin, die (traditionelle) lehrstrategien in eine Didaktik der Aneignungsstrategien zu übersetzen."[353]

The central idea is to translate traditional strategies of learning as transmission into didactics of learning as acquisition. This is open to diverse interpretation, but it is nevertheless correct: the Dalton Plan wishes to replace teaching as an effort on the part of the teacher by learning as activity on the part of the pupil. According to Popp's analysis the Dalton Plan is meanwhile for the most part a "Konzept selbstgesteuerten Lernens" (a concept of self-directed learning).[354] She goes on to express herself more accurately: it is about efficient self-direction, and so: directed and structured self-direction. In our opinion the Dalton Plan only starts to stand out

---

[349] H. Besuden, Helen Parkhursts Dalton–Plan in den Vereinigten Staaten. Oldenburg: Sussman (Diss. Köln), 1955, 14.
[350] Ibid., 14-22.
[351] Ibid., 22.
[352] Ibid., 22, 23.
[353] S. Popp, Der Dalton Plan in Theorie und Praxis. Innsbruck/Wien: Studienverlag, 1999 (Zweite Auflage), 113.
[354] Ibid.

from other forms of educational reform at the more concrete level, hence: the ways in which structuring and directing take place. So-called fundamental principles don't mean much. The transformation into working principles doesn't mean everything, albeit somewhat more.

A principled approach is customary on the European continent, but is absent in Parkhurst's case. Parkhurst is not guided by principles. She is guided by practical experience. When she describes and justifies her practice, she develops theory, of course, and she responds to others' theories. But she doesn't philosophize: she doesn't speak and justify in terms of fundamental principles. Her theory is close to practice. We have reconstructed the theory: first only relying on Parkhurst's own formulations (chapter 2), then more at length and in greater detail, after having compared it with theories that have influenced it (in the present chapter). The only principles Parkhurst acknowledges, are principles in the sense of working principles.

The original theory of Dalton education cannot be summarized by means of two or three principles. A summarizing characterization of the theory of the Dalton Plan would only be adequate when the core facets of the theory are correctly identified, and conceived in their mutual relations. Those core facets are: efficiency as the aim of organizational reform of education ('organizational' defined broadly and comprising of learning environment, class management, learning materials and didactics); enterprising living and working as educational objective and freedom and interaction of group life as organizational features which facilitate learning by experience.

References

Besuden, H.: Helen Parkhursts Dalton–Plan in den Vereinigten Staaten. Oldenburg: R. Sussman (Diss. Köln), 1955.

Bigot, L.C.T., P.A. Diels en Ph. Kohnstamm: De toekomst van ons volksonderwijs. Deel 2: Scholen met een losser klasseverband. Amsterdam: Nutsuitgeverij, 1924.

Bobbitt, F.: Twelfth Yearbook of the National Society for the Study of Education. Part I. The Supervision of City Schools. Some General Principles of Management Applied to the Problems of City-School Systems. Bloomington, Ill.: Public School Publishing, 1913.

Bobbitt, F.: The Curriculum. Boston: Houghton Mifflin Company, 1918.

Bobbitt, F.: How to make a curriculum. Boston: Houghton Mifflin Company, 1924.

Bobbitt, F.: Discovering and Formulating the Objectives of Teacher Training Institutions. Journal of Educational Research, 10, 1924, 187-196.

Bode, B.H.: Modern Educational Theories. New York: Macmillan, 1927.

Bode, B.H.: Progressive education at the cross roads. New York: Macmillan, 1938.

Bokhorst, S.C.: Individueel onderwijs en het Dalton-Plan. Rotterdam: Nijgh & Van Ditmar's Uitgevers-maatschappij, 1974.

Brooks, R.: In a world set apart: The Dalton dynasty at King Alfred School, 1920-1960. History of Education, Vol. 27, 1998, 421-440.

Callahan, R.E.: Education and the Cult of Efficiency. Chicago/London: University of Chicago Press, 1962.

Cayton, M.K.: Emerson's Emergence, Self and Society in the Transformation of New England, 1800-1845. Chapel Hill/London: University of North Carolina Press, 1989.

Conklin, E.G: Heredity and Environment in the Development of Men. Princeton: Princeton University Press, 1939. (Sixth Edition)

Cuban, L.: How Teachers Taught. New York/London: Teachers College Press, 1993. (Second Edition)

Dewey, E.: The Dalton Laboratory Plan. New York: E.P. Dutton & Company, 1922.

Dewey, J.: The University School. University (of Chicago) Record, 1, Nov. 1896. Ook in J.A. Boydston (Ed.), The early works of John Dewey, 1882-1898: Vol. 5 1895-1898: Early Essays (pp. 436-441). Carbondale/Edwardsville: Southern Illinois University Press, 1972.

Dewey, J.: Plan of Organization of the University Primary School. In J.A. Boydston (Ed.), The early works of John Dewey, 1882-1898: Vol. 5 1895-1898: Early Essays (pp. 224-243). Carbondale/Edwardsville: Southern Illinois University Press, 1972.

Dewey, J.: School and Society. Chicago/London: University of Chicago Press, 1899.

Dewey, J.: The Child and the Curriculum. Chicago/London: The University of Chicago Press, 1902.

Dewey, J.: Democracy and Education, 1916. Edition consulted: The Middle Works 1899-1924, Volume 9 1916. Edited by J.A. Boydston. Carbondale/Edwardsville: Southern Illinois University Press, 1980.

Dewey, J.: Social purposes in education. In J.A. Boydston (Ed.), The middle works of John Dewey, 1899-1924: Vol. 15 1923-1924: Journal articles, essays, and miscellany published (pp. 158-169). Carbondale/Edwardsville: Southern Illinois University Press, 1983.

Dewey, J.: The Theory of the Chicago Experiment. In K.C. Mayhew & A.C. Edwards, The Dewey School: The Laboratory School of the University of Chicago, 1896-1903. New York/London: D. Appleton Century Company, 1936.

Dewey, J.: The Chicago Experiment. In K.C. Mayhew & A.C. Edwards, The Dewey School: The Laboratory School of the University of Chicago, 1896-1903. New York/London: D. Appleton Century Company, 1936.

Dewey, J.: Experience and Education. Kappa Delta Pi, 1938. Edition consulted: New York/London: Macmillan Publishing Company, 1963.

Eichelberger, H.: Einführung. A Way of Life.. In H. Eichelberger (Hrsg.), Eine Einführung in die Daltonplan-Pädagogik. Innsbruck: StudienVerlag, 2002.

Eichelberger, H.: Der Daltonplan. In H. Eichelberger (Hrsg.), Eine Einführung in die Daltonplan-Pädagogik. Innsbruck: StudienVerlag, 2002.

Emerson, R.W.: New England Reformers. 1844. Available online: http://www.emersoncentral.com/newengland.htm.

Emerson, R.W.: Representative Men. 1850. Available online: http://www.emersoncentral.com/repmen.htm

Emerson, R.W.: On Education. Undated. Available online: http://www.vcu.edu/engweb/transcendentalism/authors/emerson/essays/education.html.

Essen, M. van & J.D. Imelman: Historische Pedagogiek. Baarn: Intro, 1999.

Faculty meeting on Philosophy and Objectives of the DALTON SCHOOL. New York: The Dalton School, 1940.

Geissler, G.: Dalton-Plan. In A. Paetz & U. Pilarczyk (Hg.): Schulen die anders waren. Berlin: Volk und Wissen Verlag, 1990.

Gutek, G.L.: The Montessori Method. Lanham etc.: Rowman & Littlefield, 2004.

Hage, D.L. and J. Jonges: Daltononderwijs op de ULOschool. Groningen: J.B. Wolters, 1962.

Hamilton, D.: Towards a theory of schooling. London/New York/Philadelphia: The Falmer Press, 1989.

Kilpatrick, W.H.: The Montessori Method examined. Boston: Houghton Mifflin Company, 1914.

Kilpatrick, W.H.: An Effort at Appraisal. In G.M. Whipple (Ed.). The Twenty-Fourth Yearbook of the National Society for the Study of Education. Part II. Adapting Schools to Individual Differences. Bloomington Ill.: NSSE, 1925.

Kimmins, C.W. and B. Rennie: The Triumph of the Dalton Plan. London: Ivor Nicholson & Watson Ltd., 1924.

Kliebard, H.M.: The struggle for the American Curriculum. New York/London, Routledge Falmer, 2004. (Third Edition)

Kohnstamm, Ph.: De nieuwe school. Groningen: Noordhoff, 1925.

Lager, D.: Helen Parkhurst and the Dalton Plan: The Life and Work of an American Educator. The University of Connecticut (Diss.), 1983.

Lillard, A.S.: Montessori. The Science behind the genius. New York: Oxford University Press, 2005.

Luke, D.R.: Champion of Children. Typescript, undated.

Luke, D.R.: Oasis for Children. Typescript, undated.

Montessori, M.: The Montessori Method. New York: Frederick a. Stokes Company, 1912.

Montessori, M.: The Montessori Elementary Material. (The Advanced Montessori Method. Part II). London: William Heinemann, 1918.

Parkhurst, H.: The Dalton Plan. Times Educational Supplement, July 2, July 9, July 16, July 23, July 30, August 6, 1921.

Parkhurst, H.: Education on the Dalton Plan. New York: E.P. Dutton & Company, 1922. Consulted: Fourth edition: 1926. (The page numbering in the various editions varies). The fourth printing is available online via www.archive.org (direct link: http://www.archive.org/details/educationondalto00parkiala).

Parkhurst, H.: The Dalton Laboratory Plan. In G.M. Whipple (Ed.). The Twenty-Fourth Yearbook of the National Society for the Study of Education. Part II. Adapting Schools to Individual Differences. Bloomington Ill.: NSSE, 1925, 83-94.

Parkhurst, H.: Exploring the Child's World. New York: Appleton-Century-Crofts, 1951.

Popp, S.: Der Dalton Plan in Theorie und Praxis. Innsbruck/Wien: Studienverlag, 1999. (Second edition)

Richardson Jr., R.D.: Emerson. The Mind on Fire. Berkeley/Los Angelos/London: University of California Press, 1995.

Röhrs, H.: Die progressive Erziehungsbewegung. Verlauf und Auswirkungen der Reformpädagogik in den USA. Hannover: Schroedel Verlag, 1977.

Semel, S.F.: The Daltonschool. The Transformation of a Progressive School. New York: Peter Lang, 1992.

Swift, E.J.: Mind in the Making. A Study in Mental Development. New York: Charles Scribner's Sons, 1908.

Taylor, F.W.: The principles of scientific management. New York: Harper and Brothers, 1911.

Taylor, F.W.: Shop Management. New York: Harper and Brothers, 1912.

Washburne, C.W.: Burk's individual system as developed at Winnetka. In G.M. Whipple (Ed.). The Twenty-Fourth Yearbook of the National Society for the Study of Education. Part II. Adapting Schools to Individual Differences. Bloomington Ill.: NSSE, 1925.

www.ingramcontent.com/pod-product-compliance
Lightning Source LLC
Chambersburg PA
CBHW070809230426
43665CB00017B/2539